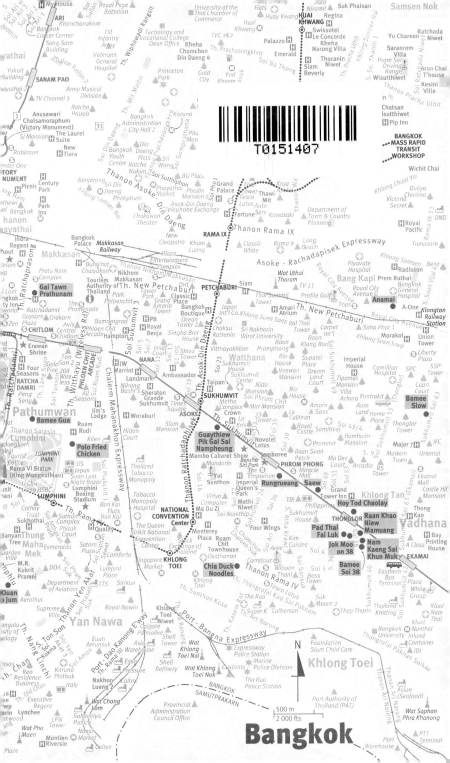

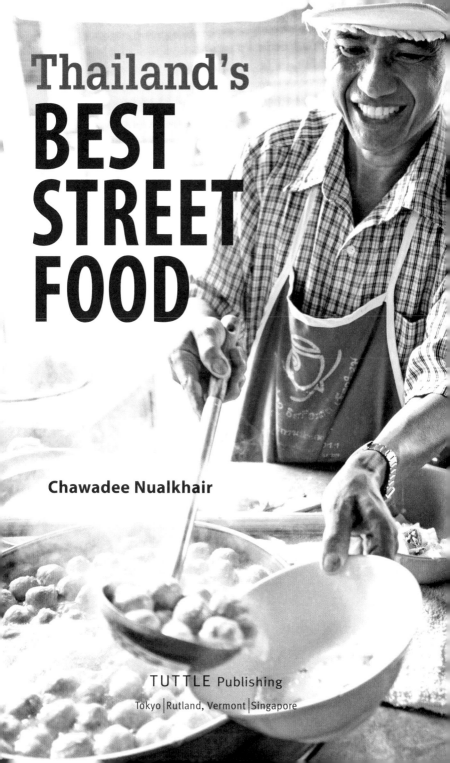

Thailand's
BEST
STREET
FOOD

Chawadee Nualkhair

TUTTLE Publishing

Tokyo | Rutland, Vermont | Singapore

Contents

Recipes

Introduction
Is Street Food Dying Out?

A few months ago, a friend said to me that Thai street food would most likely be around for only another "10 to 15 years". This statement surprised me but I really couldn't argue with him. International food chains have mushroomed in most of Bangkok's urban centers offering cheap and affordable foreign specialties such as hamburgers and Japanese curry rice, and Thais aren't resisting them. In fact, Thais—to use the slogan of one popular fast food franchise—"are loving

it". A study published in the *Journal of Health Science* in early 2012 indicated that Western fast food is one of the top ten snacks most commonly eaten by Thai children. The reasons for this are many, but they all boil down to the fact that international fast food has become more readily available and costs only slightly more than Thai food on offer at the average food stall down the street.

I am not really bemoaning the globalizaton of Thai diets. It's true that, for many people, street food and fast food are interlinked—nourishment meant to be grabbed quickly on the way somewhere, when one is too hungry to wait for something better. After all, street food blossomed in just this way. It was initially sold as quick noodle snacks for those on the go by enterprising Thai-Chinese vendors along Bangkok's many canals, and then became popular for harried parents who needed to buy quick dinners on their way home from work.

Street food in Thailand has grown into a fairly substantial business, possibly grossing as much as 800 billion baht a year, according to very rough estimates from JP Morgan. However, Thai street food—like much of Thai culture in general—has shown an amazing ability to adapt and absorb influences which would threaten to engulf lesser entities. I like to compare it to "High Street" fashion, the lower-priced styles that the average person wears. Many times, the High

HEALTH CONCERNS

In today's world, no kind of dining is without its risks. Street food obviously carries with it its own set of issues, so buyer beware. For this reason, I have tried as best as I can to stick to long-standing street food vendors with good reputations. Focus on well-established places with high turnover and try to avoid raw seafood or meat. Vendors are periodically tested by city authorities for cleanliness. The ones that pass muster are marked by a green and blue "Clean Food Good Taste" badge issued by the Bangkok administration.

Street is influenced by haute couture just as Thai street food has been influenced by more expensive restaurants. For example, the coconut milk-based curries of the common *khao gub gaeng* (rice with curry) stall did, after all, originate in far grander kitchens.

Thai street food has moved well beyond noodles and curries to encompass an extensive range of snacks, salads, soups, sweets and heartier wok-fried noodle- and rice-based dishes. All incorporate a diverse array of ingredients, from regional favorites such as the Northern Thai sour fermented sausage known as *naem* to newfangled concoction like instant noodles. Some have even taken their cue from foreign cuisines, presenting *takoyaki* (fried octopus balls), a mutant Thai take on sushi, or standard Western favorites like beef stroganoff, for a third of the price. And, yes, sometimes

High Street does inspire haute couture if the recent spate of upscale restaurants featuring Isaan food, once derided as a "low-class" street staple, is anything to go by. It is difficult to ascertain a more precise figure as many of the stalls are unregulated and thus form part of the shadow economy.

So what do I think about my friend's prediction? In Thailand, there will always be a market for well-made cheap food in an informal setting without bells and whistles, such as air-conditioning, proper chairs or even tables. Thais have long shown that they are willing to withstand any sort of inconvenience in the pursuit of something culinary, provided it is worth it. I believe that fifteen years from now, Thai street food may look different and may comprise different dishes but it will definitely still be delicious and will remain uniquely Thai.

Types of Thai Street Food

There is, and always has been, a great deal of debate on what street food is.
For some, it must be something sold directly from a cart or table set out on the sidewalk; for others, it is nothing more than food sold from any open-air place (or, as the Bangkok Metropolitan Administration puts it, an establishment with "no more than three walls").

My view on this matter falls somewhere in the middle. Many open-air Thai eateries are nothing less than full-fledged restaurants serving a wide range of dishes from an extensive menu, while other shophouses specialize in a specific dish or niche of Thai food.

1 Mobile

The standard idea of a typical street food vendor is mobility. These vendors usually operate from a single mobile cart that specializes in takeaway or a cart with tables set up around it. Occasionally, the vendor sells his or her wares from a pole with baskets fixed to either end or from a table placed on the sidewalk. The vendor may sell from either a fixed location or move around from time to time. They normally specialize in one dish or in one type of food, such as Isaan, or Northeastern Thai food.

2 Made-to-order

These *aharn tham sung* vendors operate from fixed locations, usually out of a shophouse. They make a variety of dishes but generally rely on a fixed repertoire of specialties. Some of the very best (these are usually characterized by the baskets of fresh ingredients on display in front of their woks) make whatever you request or are able to make up dishes depending on what ingredients you select.

3 Shophouse

Vendors selling food from a shophouse are usually the most successful and oldest in their trade. Many vendors start from carts and eventually work their way up to a shophouse that is able to accommodate more guests and provide the vendor with better cooking space. They generally stick to their original specialties but from time to time branch out into other dishes that are related in some way to the specialty that made them famous. The most successful vendors move on from shophouses to adjacent air-conditioned rooms and, eventually, open up full-fledged restaurants.

4 Curry rice

The *khao gub gaeng* (also *khao raad gaeng*) vendor's cart or table has a selection of ready-made curries and stir-fries displayed in front of the vendor. Curries and stir-fries may change from day to day but the vendor usually has a specialty that never changes. Customers simply point to what they want and it is either served on a plate of rice or placed in a clear plastic bag for taking home.

How to Use This Book

Street food is a serious matter to a lot of people. Many normally laid-back and happy-go-lucky people can get pretty hot under the collar when the conversation takes a culinary turn. Debates over the best places to grab a bowl of noodles or even what does or does not constitute a street food stall can easily devolve into impassioned free-for-alls. To make things easy (for myself) and to reduce the number of irate emails about this or that street food vendor, I would like to set out my criteria for what constitutes a street food stall, how I make the selections for this book, and the purpose I hope the book serves.

The Purpose of This Book

This book started from the feeling of intimidation I had when I moved to Thailand nearly 20 years ago and contemplated buying a street food meal on my own. Not knowing the language as well as I should, I was unsure about what to order, what I'd actually be getting and how to ensure I got what I wanted with as little fuss as possible.

This guide seeks to address those issues while focusing on long-standing and relatively hygienic vendors who enjoy a high turnover. In other words, the stalls I have selected are almost all famous in one way or another. There may well be a great fried noodle stall tucked away somewhere in a corner of Chinatown that has better food, but if it is obscure or relatively new, it could easily move to another location or simply cease operating altogether, hence my focus on the older, more established street food purveyors. I also find the better known stalls are the most patronized ones, and I like the idea of a quick turnover of

ingredients. This cuts down on the chance of items being left to "stew" in the open for hours, if not days.

Ultimately, this book is meant to help street food newbies who are unsure about street food but who still want to share in something that is undoubtedly a huge part of Thai dining culture. There is no need to stick to big restaurants or to cower in one's hotel coffee shop. On the other end of the spectrum, long-time street food aficionados may also come across something in these pages for them: a reminder of a long-forgotten favorite or a vendor or two who serves a beloved dish in an unfamiliar town. I hope they, too, will find this book useful.

What is a Street Food Stall?

The Bangkok Metropolitan Administration recognizes two types of vendors: mobile vendors who sell from carts or carry their wares slung on a pole across their backs, and fixed vendors who sell from a stall, usually extending from a house or in a shophouse. These fixed locations are defined as places with no more than three permanent walls. I am being unusually detailed about this because most of the stalls in this book are of the shophouse variety. I have also added other criteria which I hope will separate these vendors from open-air restaurants that also operate out of shophouses:

1 **There must be one or, at most, two specialties "of the house"**

2 **The kitchen must be located in front of the dining area, in full view of the diners**

I like the more flexible approach to characterizing street food stalls because many vendors, after having spent years building up a reputation from their mobile carts, have moved to fixed locations and may have opened either full-fledged restaurants (see Polo Fried Chicken, p. 71) or other branches (see Bamee Sawang, p. 57). That is the story of street food. The good ones flourish and sometimes expand. Others have to move to a location that may serve them better. The good thing about Thailand is that there is always a place somewhere for an enterprising food vendor. You may find that places that are clearly street food stalls are not included. This is because they are either *aharn tham sung* (made-to-order) stalls or *khao gub gaeng* (curry rice) stalls which feature pre-made curries. There are simply too many of these to include.

Choosing the Stalls

I spent many months eating at the stalls featured in the book so the basic answer to the question of choice has to be "I like the food at these places." But there are other criteria. In Bangkok, for instance, I focused on neighborhoods that I knew well, hence the exclusion of important areas like Victory Monument and Ari. I didn't want to include stalls just for the sake of including them even if they were located in well-known neighborhoods.

In the provinces, I focused on regional specialties and dishes that are harder to find. I wanted to showcase the diversity inherent in Thai food as well as show

off the different characteristics of each region. You may find that, as in Bangkok, your favorite neighborhood or city is not included. The reason is because I have but one humble stomach and have a limited amount of time on this good green earth. It is a work in progress. Maybe some day I will be able to provide a wider coverage.

The whole premise of this book is that no two vendors are created equal. Egg noodles aren't the same wherever you go. The same applies to chicken rice or duck noodles or any other street food dish you may favor. This is why (with the exclusion of Sukhumvit Soi 38, which is special) I do not focus on well-known street food areas. The vendors are simply not all of the same standard. If the "neighborhood/night market/walking street approach" is your favorite way of exploring street food, then by all means go ahead. You will not need this book to do it. What I do hope is that this book ends up inspiring you to hit the pavement and explore, not just the places in the book but whatever it is that may strike your fancy—just eat it.

I want discussions, questions, heated exchanges. Readers of my first book have given me feedback, both good and bad, on all the Bangkok vendors. That feedback invariably makes me happy even though it is occasionally negative, because it means the book has, in some small way, contributed to each reader's search to discover what they love and what works for them.

NOODLES IN SOUP

First brought to Thailand by Chinese immigrants, this "Chinese fast food" has morphed into a suprisingly wide variety of dishes based on:

1 Types of noodles

2 Main ingredients (proteins) with the noodles

3 Styles of broth

4 Whether you want your noodles with or without broth

Types of Noodles

Bamee บะหมี่

Chinese-style egg and wheat flour noodles

Giem ee เกี้ยมอี๋

A type of hand-rolled Chinese noodle resembling spaetzle

Giew เกี๊ยว

Wonton, usually filled with a type of pork stuffing

Guay jab ก๋วยจั๊บ

A type of hand-rolled longer Chinese noodle always served in a pork broth

Sen lek เส้นเล็ก

Thinner, flat noodles made from rice flour

Sen mee เส้นหมี่

Rice vermicelli—tiny angel hair-like noodles made from rice flour

Sen yai เส้นใหญ่

Wide noodles made from rice flour

Sieng hai เซี่ยงไฮ้

Green hand-rolled Chinese noodles

Wunsen วุ้นเส้น

Glass vermicelli noodles made from mung beans

Main Ingredients

Guay jab ก๋วยจั๊บ
Choice of clear or cloudy pork broth always accompanying hand-rolled Chinese noodles

Han ห่าน
Goose (served roasted)

Moo หมู
Pork (served as meatballs, barbecued, sliced or as mince)

Nam sai น้ำใส
Clear broth

Nam tok or leuat น้ำตก
Includes animal blood

Nuea เนื้อ
Beef (served stewed, freshly boiled or as meatballs)

Ped เป็ด
Duck (served roasted)

Phae แพะ
Goat (served roasted or braised)

Styles of Broth

Pla ปลา
Fish (served freshly boiled or as meatballs)

Talay ทะเล
Mixed seafood (usually shrimp, squid and fish)

Tom yum ต้มยำ
Like the soup, a spicy lemongrass-infused flavor

Taohu เต้าหู้
Tofu, usually deep-fried into a type of meatball

Yen ta fo เย็นตาโฟ
Red fermented tofu sauce accompanying seafood noodles

FRIED NOODLES
ก๋วยเตี๋ยวผัด

Noodles are not only served in soup. They are also fried in a variety of styles. Most food stalls will specialize in one or two types of fried noodle. The dishes are usually eaten with a fork and spoon.

Khanom jeen
ขนมจีน

This fermented rice noodle is often mistaken for a Chinese dish because its name mistakenly translates into "Chinese candy". It is, in fact, of Mon origin and is served alongside a variety of curries, the best known being *nam prik* (chili sauce), *gaeng kiew waan* (sweet green curry) and *nam ya* (fish curry). *Khanom jeen* is usually available at a *khao gub gaeng* (rice curry) stand.

Pad kee mow
ผัดขี้เมา

Known familiarly as "drunken noodles", these noodles are fried with a variety of spices and are typically ordered after a big night out when the diner has indulged in a few too many drinks. Served with a protein (pork, chicken, seafood or beef), the dish is usually available at *aharn tham sung* (made-to-order) stalls.

Pad Thai
ผัดไทย

The best-known type of fried noodle dish, the noodles here include both Chinese and Thai elements, such as rice noodles, tamarind juice and shrimp. Diners can usually opt for *pad Thai* with or without egg. *Pad Thai* vendors usually also serve *hoy tod*, a type of oyster-topped omelet or eggy crepe.

Rad na/Pad see ew
ราดหน้า/ผัดซีอิ๊ว

Served with pork, chicken, seafood or beef, these rice flour noodles are fried and then covered in a thick gravy. The same stalls that serve *rad na* usually serve *pad see ew*, or rice noodles fried with soy sauce and some form of protein (pork, chicken, seafood or beef).

RICE DISHES
อาหารประเภทข้าว

Rice, or *khao*, forms the backbone of Thai cuisine so it's no surprise that it features prominently in street food. The following are the best-known types of rice dishes available:

Jok โจ๊ก
This Chinese-style rice porridge features smaller rice kernels and a thicker consistency than the Thai variation. It is usually accompanied by slivered ginger, green onion, pork meatballs, liver and/or innards. A half-cooked egg is optional as is the accompanying *patongo* (deep-fried dough).

Khao ka moo ข้าวขาหมู
Rice served with a fatty, braised pork leg accompanied by braised leafy greens and a sour, vinegary chili sauce to cut the fatty aftertaste.

Khao man gai ข้าวมันไก่
A Thai-Chinese dish, steamed chicken with fatty rice is served with a clear broth and at least one form of chili-spiked brown bean sauce.

Khao mok gai
ข้าวหมกไก่
Loosely translated as "chicken buried in a mountain of rice", this Thai-Muslim chicken dish usually features a chicken leg accompanied by rice colored yellow by turmeric, topped with deep-fried shallots and a spicy-tart chicken broth.

Khao na ped/moo
ข้าวหน้าเป็ด/หมู
Rice topped with barbecued duck or pork. Both are usually served at the same food stall.

Khao niew gai yang/gai tod
ข้าวเหนียวไก่ย่าง/ไก่ทอด
This Northeastern Thai dish comprises sticky rice accompanied by barbecued or fried chicken and, usually, *som tum* (green papaya salad). It is among the more popular street food options in Bangkok.

Khao pad
ข้าวผัด
Fried rice, usually served as part of an *aharn tham sung* cart but occasionally offered by noodle vendors to placate customers who either want something extra or aren't in the mood for noodles.

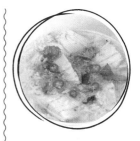

Khao tom
ข้าวต้ม
This Thai rice porridge is either served plain with a number of small side dishes or with a variety of proteins included in the broth (usually fish, assorted seafood, pork or chicken).

APPETIZERS AND SNACKS
อาหารว่าง

Thais are often described as "inveterate snackers" and their fondness for grazing usually leads them to one of these types of snacks between meals:

Guaythiew lod
ก๋วยเตี๋ยวหลอด
Another type of flat noodle, this one is stuffed with pork or seafood and drizzled with a delicious sauce. The best examples of this are found in Chinatown.

Hoy tod
หอยทอด
Oysters fried in omelet, served with a sweet red chili sauce. These vendors usually also serve *pad Thai*.

Khanom jeeb
ขนมจีบ
These steamed Chinese dumplings include pork and seafood. The best examples can be found throughout Chinatown.

Krapho pla
กระเพาะปลา
Fish maw soup. The best examples are again found in Chinatown.

Nuea khem
เนื้อเค็ม
Translated as "salty beef", this form of beef jerky—traditionally dried in the sun—is usually eaten with sticky rice. It keeps well.

Samosa
ซาโมซ่า
The Indian deep-fried dumpling with a savory, tart stuffing. Also sometimes accompanied by *tikki*, a deep-fried soft patty with a spicy stuffing.

Satay
สะเต๊ะ
Available as pork or chicken, the protein is grilled on a bamboo skewer and coated with coconut milk. It is accompanied by peanut sauce and a cucumber and shallot relish.

DESSERTS

ของหวาน

Thais are known to harbor a fondness for sweets so it's no surprise that street food desserts abound.

Bamee wan
บะหมี่หวาน
Egg noodles served with an assortment of Thai-Chinese delicacies in syrup and topped with shaved ice.

Bua loy kai waan
บัวลอยไข่หวาน
Translated as "floating lotus sweet egg", these dumplings are served in heated coconut milk with an egg or egg white.

Bua loy nam khing
บัวลอยน้ำขิง
Translated as "floating lotus with ginger water", this Chinese dessert comprises dumplings stuffed with ground sesame seeds served in a sweet, invigorating ginger syrup.

Chao guay
เฉาก๊วย

This Chinese jelly, served in a syrup with ice, is reminiscent of sweetened black coffee and is a light, refreshing treat at the end of a big meal.

Khanom bueang
ขนมเบื้อง

These interesting taco-like desserts mix elements of the sweet with the savory.

Khao niew mamuang
ข้าวเหนียวมะม่วง

Sticky rice with mango and coconut milk. One of Thailand's best-loved desserts.

Lotchong
ลอดช่อง

These green "tapioca squiggles" are served in an iced coconut milk broth.

Pae guay
แปะก๊วย

Yellow gingko nuts can be served alone, hot or cold, in a syrup or even part of a Thai-style shaved ice "buffet". The Chinese have tradition-ally believed this dessert helps promote brain function.

Roti
โรตี

Like their Indian counterparts, these are flat breads but are flakier and served with a variety of sweet toppings, such as banana or condensed milk and sugar.

BEVERAGES
เครื่องดื่ม

You will typically find one or more of the following beverages at a street stall:

Cha dum yen ชาดำเย็น
Black iced tea

Cha manao ชามะนาว
Iced lemon tea

Cha yen ชาเย็น
Iced milk tea

Gafae yen กาแฟเย็น
Iced coffee

Geck huay yen เก๊กฮวยเย็น
Iced chrysanthemum tea

Lorhangguay หล่อฮั้งก้วย
Chinese herbal beverage

Nam atlom น้ำอัดลม
Soft drink/carbonated beverage

Nam bai bua bok น้ำใบบัวบก
Pennywort juice

Nam baitoey น้ำใบเตย
Pandanus leaf juice

Nam buai น้ำบ๊วย
Pickled plum juice

Nam dok anchan น้ำดอกอัญชัญ
Butterfly pea juice

Nam farang น้ำฝรั่ง
Guava juice

Nam khaeng น้ำแข็ง
Ice

Nam krajiep น้ำกระเจี๊ยบ
Roselle juice (sometimes referred to
as hibiscus juice)

Nam lamyai น้ำลำไย
Longan juice

Nam manao น้ำมะนาว
Lime juice

Nam maphrao น้ำมะพร้าว
Coconut juice

Nam matum น้ำมะตูม
Bael fruit juice

Nam plao น้ำเปล่า
Fresh water/drinking water

Nam saowarot น้ำเสาวรส
Passionfruit juice

Nam som น้ำส้ม
Orange juice

Nam takrai น้ำตะไคร้
Lemongrass juice

Olieng โอเลี้ยง
Chinese-style black iced coffee

Bangkok

Chinatown · Banglamphu · Hualamphong
Silom/Sathorn · Sukhumvit · Other Areas

The Thai capital is the center of the country's street food world and is the point from which the country's culinary trends flow. From char-grilled Isaan-style meat to fried noodles bathed in seafood gravy, Thailand's best street food dishes can be found in this metropolis, and for the most part with minimal effort. The trick lies in determining which of the city's numerous food stalls are worth patronizing.

Over time, Bangkok has served as the setting for most of Thailand's major culinary developments, be it the growth of the industry on the backs of Thai-Chinese vendors during the reign of King Rama IV, the street food boom after the widespread incorporation of women into the workplace or the recent inclusion of "foreign" street foods in the culinary lexicon. As a result, there are an estimated 500,000 street food stalls set up at 683 points in 50 districts of the city.

How the food stalls in this book were selected
A good number of the stands offer the standard fare consumed by Thais: juices, sliced fruit and soft drinks/carbonated beverages. Basic dishes, such as grilled bananas, omelets and pickled fruits, are also hawked daily. These types of stalls are not included in this book because one could conceivably pass for another. Because of the massive number of establishments in Bangkok, only well-known locations for street food are included, with some exceptions made for food stalls in areas not particularly known for their outstanding food.

LEFT: Sukhothai noodles at Somsong Pochana, Banglamphu

Bangkok's Best Street Food Districts
These are the best street food areas in the city to explore

CHINATOWN (YAOWARAJ)
This is Bangkok's best-known street food area. Holding fast to its identity as the originator of Bangkok street food, Yaowaraj (also spelt Yaowarat) offers a dizzying array of specialties, most of which are Chinese or Thai-Chinese. Go at night-time to see the street food scene come alive. Adjacent to Chinatown is "Little India" or Pahurat.

BANGLAMPHU
Sometimes regarded as a tourist zone because of its proximity to Khao Sarn Road, this part of town offers many Thai, Thai-Chinese and Thai-Muslim specialties with a dash of "old city" atmosphere. For diners eager to witness this charm together with seriously delicious food, Banglamphu can't be beaten.

HUALAMPHONG (SAM YAN)
One of the older street food areas in Bangkok, this collection of street corners, which includes a well-known wet market

that was recently renovated, offers great diversity for the adventurous gourmet.

SILOM/SATHORN
Bangkok's Central Business District is chock-a-block with lunchtime streetside spots catering to the voracious and varied appetites of the typical Thai office worker. Night-time draws a different, more eclectic, crowd.

SUKHUMVIT
Bangkok's monied residential district encompasses a mix of wealthy Thais and expats. Although dominated by upscale European restaurants and fast food joints, this major thoroughfare also is home to food stalls that hawk some delectable Thai and Thai-Chinese specialties.

OTHER AREAS
You might consider yourself in the middle of nowhere, but you can be certain there is a delicious reason as to why you are trekking there.

Bangkok Chinatown's Yaowaraj Road at night

Chinatown (YAOWARAJ)

Bangkok's Chinatown—or what the locals call "Yaowaraj"—epitomizes the hustle and bustle, fun and chaos and smells, sights and sounds of Thai street food 24 hours a day. From early in the morning when the curry rice vendors start hawking their wares and the market vendors begin to set up shop, until late in the evening when the rice porridge shops and streetside seafood restaurants rule the roost, Chinatown is a simmering cauldron of culinary activity.

Despite the widespread assimilation of the ethnic Chinese in Thailand, Chinatown has retained a strong Chinese identity. Made up largely of Hokkien and Teochew, the Thai-Chinese population has grown by leaps and bounds since the 1700s when the seeds of Bangkok's Chinatown were first sown. Yaowaraj (or Yaowarat) Road, Chinatown's main thoroughfare, was built in 1891 during the reign of King Rama V, who also gave the neighborhood the name Yaowaraj, which means "young king".

Today, Chinatown is still known as a major center of commerce for food items and Chinese goods. Tuk-tuk still ply the roads that wind through the area, Chinese opera can still be heard some evenings and local residents continue to line up for their favorite street food snacks after work or school. For lovers of Thai street food, a visit to this part of town is a must.

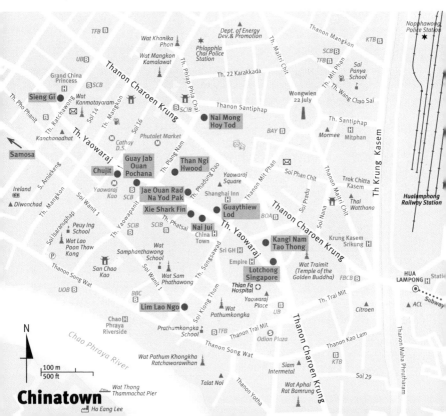

Chinatown

Guaythiew Lod

ก๋วยเตี๋ยวหลอด, ถนนเยาวราช หน้าร้านนาฬิกาไซโก้ที่อยู่ข้างร้านหูฉลามสกาลา

STREETSIDE CART, YAOWARAJ ROAD, CHINATOWN

Despite its humble appearance, this stall serves among the best stuffed flat noodles in the city: rice noodles smothered under a blanket of bean sprouts, pork, calamari and shiitake mushrooms, soaked in a delicious soy-based sauce.

GETTING THERE

In front of the Seiko watch shop and next to Hu Chalaam Scala
Tel 02-225-3558, 081-559-8339
Open 18.30–1.00 except Monday

SPECIALTY

Flat noodles stuffed with pork (*guaythiew lod*), 35 baht
ก๋วยเตี๋ยวหลอดกับหมู

OPTIONS

With egg (*sai kai*), without egg (*mai kai*), extra pork (*moo piset*)

NOTABLE EXTRAS

Fish maw soup (*krapho pla*), 50–100 baht (depending on size)

STANDARD TOPPINGS

Bean sprouts, scallions, deep-fried garlic

BEVERAGES

Fresh water (*nam plao*), iced chrysanthemum tea (*geck huay yen*), 10 baht

SEATING Yes

ON THE TABLE

Chopsticks, forks and spoons, condiment tray, vinegar with peppers, Chinese black vinegar (*zisho*)

RESTROOM No

Best for **SNACKS**

Nai Jui

นายจุ้ย ข้าวหมูแดงหมูกรอบ, ถนนเยาวราช ข้างร้านเชี้ยหูฉลาม

STREETSIDE CART, YAOWARAJ ROAD, CHINATOWN

Delicious (and naturally crispy) pork atop soft, fluffy rice and slathered in a thick, sweet sauce—what could be better? This stand offers a great example of this dish, plus its kissing cousins—barbecued pork and braised pork leg—all great celebrations of the pig on a plate.

GETTING THERE

On the Old Market side of Yaowaraj Road, a few feet from Xie Shark Fin
Tel 081-009-9746, 086-127-2666
Open 8.30–1.00 except Monday

SPECIALTY
Rice topped with crispy pork (*khao moo grob*), 35–50 baht (depending on how many boiled egg halves and how much pork)
ข้าวหมูกรอบ

OPTIONS
With egg (*sai kai*), without egg (*mai kai*), extra pork (*moo piset*)

NOTABLE EXTRAS
Rice topped with red barbecued pork (*khao moo daeng*), 35–50 baht; rice with fatty pork leg (*khao ka moo*), 35–50 baht

STANDARD TOPPINGS
Side of sliced cucumber

BEVERAGES
Chinese-style black iced coffee (*olieng*), black iced tea (*cha dum yen*), iced chrysan-themum tea (*geck huay yen*), cocoa, longan juice (*nam lamyai*), roselle juice (*nam krajiep*), 10 baht

SEATING Yes

ON THE TABLE
Spring onions, sweet soy sauce, sliced chilies in vinegar, pounded chilies in vinegar, sugar, chili powder

RESTROOM No

Best for CRISPY PORK

Xie Shark Fin

เซี้ยหูฉลาม, ถนนเยาวราช ข้างร้านทองใบเยาวราช

STREETSIDE CART, YAOWARAJ ROAD, CHINATOWN

Yet another option in the wildly diverse world of noodles:
Hong Kong-style egg noodles that resemble spaghetti,
only thinner. This vendor serves up some consistently delicious
examples of these noodles.

GETTING THERE

On the Old Market side of Yaowaraj
Road, next to Tong Bai Yaowaraj
Tel 081-889-6976
Open 19.00–1.00 except Monday

SPECIALTY

"Hong Kong" fried egg
noodles with crab, shrimp and
chicken (*bamee hong kong*),
65 baht
บะหมี่ฮ่องกง

OPTIONS

Without crab (*mai pu*), shrimp
(*mai goong*) and/or chicken
(*mai gai*)

NOTABLE EXTRAS

Fish maw soup (*krapho pla*),
60 baht; shark's fin soup
(*hu chalam*), 300–500 baht
(depending on size of fin)

STANDARD TOPPINGS

(for Hong Kong noodles)
Shredded cabbage, spring
onions, bean sprouts

BEVERAGES

Cold tea water (*nam cha yen*),
2 baht; iced chrysanthemum
tea (*geck huay yen*), longan
juice (*nam lamyai*), 10 baht

SEATING Yes

ON THE TABLE

Condiment tray with black
Chinese vinegar (*zisho*), white
pepper, chili powder, toothpicks

RESTROOM No

Best for FRIED NOODLES

31

Jae Ouan Rad Na Yod Pak

เจ๊อ้วนราดหน้ายอดผัก, ถนนเยาวราช หน้าร้านนาฬิการาโด

STREETSIDE CART, YAOWARAJ ROAD, CHINATOWN

Bring your own tissues and an empty bladder to this unpretentious spot on the main thoroughfare in Bangkok's Chinatown. This vendor serves up some of the best gravy noodles in the city.

GETTING THERE

On Yaowaraj Road, in front of a Rado Citizen watch shop, on the Plang Nam Road side of the street
Tel 081-552-9882, 081-633-5102
Open 17.30–2.00 daily

SPECIALTY

Fried noodles in gravy with pork and Chinese kale, 30–50 baht (depending on options); fried noodles with soy sauce 50–60 baht (depending on options)
ราดหน้าหมูยอดผักคะน้า

OPTIONS

- For noodles in gravy (*guay-thiew rard na*): with egg (*sai kai*), rice vermicelli (*sen mee*), wide noodles (*sen yai*)
- For soy sauce noodles (*guay thiew pad see ew*): with egg (*sai kai*), rice vermicelli (*sen mee*), wide noodles (*sen yai*)

NOTABLE EXTRAS

Stir-fried Chinese kale (*pad pak kanaa*), 100 baht

STANDARD TOPPINGS

Stir-fried Chinese kale

BEVERAGES

Cold Chinese herbal water (*nam jub liang*), iced chrysanthemum tea (*geck huay yen*), 30 baht; fresh water (*nam plao*), 10 baht; orange juice (*nam som*), big bottle, 80 baht; longan juice, (*nam lamyai*), 30 baht; soft drink/carbonated beverage (*nam atlom*), 10 baht

SEATING Yes

ON THE TABLE

Forks and spoons, condiment tray, white pepper

RESTROOM No

Chujit

บัวลอยชูจิต, ถนนเยาวราช หน้าร้านทองเซ่งเฮงหลี

STREETSIDE CART, YAOWARAJ ROAD, CHINATOWN

This streetside stall may not look like much but it serves up some of the best black grass jelly and black sesame-stuffed dumplings in the city. Try with gingko nuts donated by the nearby bird's nest (*rang nok*) vendor.

GETTING THERE

On the Old Market side of Yaowaraj Road, in front of Seng Heng Lee Goldsmith
Tel 081-860-1053
Open 18.30–23.30 daily

SPECIALTY

Sesame-filled dumplings in ginger broth (*bua loy nam khing*), 30 baht; black grass jelly with shaved ice and syrup (*chao guay*), 15 baht

บัวลอยน้ำขิง เฉาก๊วย

OPTIONS

For black grass jelly: with gingko nuts (*pae guay*), 30 baht; gingko nuts only, 50 baht

NOTABLE EXTRAS

Ginger broth with tofu and fried dough, 15 baht

BEVERAGES

Chrysanthemum tea (*geck huay*), Chinese herbal beverage (*lorhangguay*), 20 baht; tofu milk (*nam taohu*), 10 baht

SEATING Yes

ON THE TABLE

Nothing but what you order

RESTROOM No

Best for
DESSERTS

Than Ngi Hwood

ตั้งหงีฮวดข้าวต้มเป็ด, 49 ซอยแปลงนาม ถ้ามาจากถนนเยาวราช อยู่ฝั่งขวา

SHOPHOUSE, 49 PLANG NAM ROAD, CHINATOWN

This shophouse serves a culinary rarity: duck rice porridge, a delicious and surprisingly light concoction that is heavy on the pepper and easy on the grease. While the atmosphere may be a bit solemn, the service is quietly solicitous.

GETTING THERE

On the right-hand side of the road if coming from Yaowaraj Road
Tel 02-227-6457, 086-751-9262
Open 10.00–21.00 daily

SPECIALTY
Duck porridge, 30 baht, 40 baht (extra duck). Extras: pork maw soup (*krapho moo*), 40 baht
ข้าวต้มเป็ด

OPTIONS
Extra duck (*piset*), no duck blood (*mai sai lued ped*), no rice, only broth (*gow low*)

STANDARD TOPPINGS
Coriander, cubed duck blood, deep-fried garlic, pickled cabbage

BEVERAGES
Fresh water (*nam plao*), 10 baht; soft drink/carbonated beverage (*nam atlom*), 8 baht; Singha beer, 70 baht; Heineken beer, 80 baht; ice, 2 baht

SEATING Yes

ON THE TABLE
Toothpicks, fish sauce, vinegar with chilies, white pepper

Best for DUCK PORRIDGE

RESTROOM
Western toilet, bowl of water to flush, no paper

34

Guay Jab Ouan Pochana

ก๋วยจั๊บอ้วนโภชนา, ถนนเยาวราช หน้าโรงภาพยนตร์รามา

SHOPHOUSE, YAOWARAJ ROAD, CHINATOWN

Located in a former movie theater, this no-frills spot attracts a large night-time crowd with its brand of flat rice noodles in a clear, peppery pork broth. Try to arrive early to snag a table close to the chef (the man behind the steaming pile of pork trimmings).

GETTING THERE

In front of the Chinatown Rama movie theater on Yaowaraj Road
Open 18.00–3.00 daily

SPECIALTY

Hand-rolled Chinese noodles in pork broth (clear broth version), 30 baht; special serving or without noodles (*gow low*), 40 baht
ก๋วยจั๊บน้ำใส

OPTIONS

Pork (*moo*), pork entrails (*krueang nai*), without noodles (*gow low*)

NOTABLE EXTRAS

Rice, 5 baht

BEVERAGES

Chinese herbal beverage (*lorhangguay*), 15 baht; iced chrysanthemum tea (*geck huay yen*), longan juice (*nam lamyai*), lotus root juice (*nam rak bua*), 10 baht

SEATING Yes

ON THE TABLE

Condiment tray

RESTROOM

Squat toilet, no paper. Entrance fee of 5 baht, located upstairs, must walk down a dark hallway and unlock the padlocked door to enter

Best for
NOODLES
SOUP

Lotchong Singapore

ลอดช่องสิงคโปร์, 680–682 สามแยกเจริญกรุง ตรงข้ามธนาคารเอเชีย (ยูโอบี)

SHOPHOUSE, 680–682 SAM YAAK CHAROEN KRUNG, CHINATOWN

This dessert vendor shares a space with a pork meatball noodle vendor. The *lotchong*, or green tapioca flour squiggles in coconut milk with shaved ice, is exemplary, an echo of the sweet treat all Thais loved as children.

GETTING THERE

Across from the Asia Bank (UOB Bank) in Sam Yaak Charoen Krung
Tel 2-221-579430
Open 11.00–23.30 except Thursday

SPECIALTY

Green tapioca squiggles (*lotchong*) in coconut milk with shaved ice, 18 baht
ลอดช่อง

BEVERAGES

Iced ginseng tea (*cha som yen*), 6 baht

SEATING Yes

ON THE TABLE

Condiment tray (for pork meatball noodles)

RESTROOM

Squat toilet, no paper

Best for DESSERTS

Nai Mong Hoy Tod

นายหมงหอยทอด, 539 ซอยพลับพลาไชย ถ้ามาจากเจริญกรุงอยู่ฝั่งขวา

SHOPHOUSE, 539 SOI PRAPACHAI, CHINATOWN

This hole-in-the-wall off Chinatown's main drag may serve the very best oyster omelets in the city. Nai Mong can be a pleasure to visit as long as you sit far from the sweltering heat of the frying station.

GETTING THERE

Walk down Plang Nam Road, cross Charoen Krung Road and go about 50 meters down Soi Prapachai until you see the sign for Nai Mong on your right
Tel 089-773-3133, 02-623-1890
Open 11.00–21.30 daily

SPECIALTY
Oyster or mussel omelets, 65 baht
หอยแมงภู่และหอยนางรมทอด

OPTIONS
Oyster (*hoy nangrom*) or mussel (*hoy mangpu*); soft (*nim*) or crispy (*grob*)

NOTABLE EXTRAS
Crab fried rice (*kha pad pu*), 60 baht

BEVERAGES
Fresh water (*nam plao*), Coke, Sprite, 10 baht; Splash orange, 15 baht

SEATING Yes

ON THE TABLE
Chopsticks, forks and spoons, fish sauce, white pepper

RESTROOM
Western toilet, bucket of water to flush, no paper

Best for SNACKS

Kangi Nam Tao Thong

คันกี่ น้ำเต้าทอง, 676 สามแยกเจริญกรุง

SHOPHOUSE, 676 CHAROEN KRUNG ROAD, CHINATOWN

This is no typical streetside stand. Instead, locals treat it like a drug store, and the steady stream of customers well into the evening attests to the efficacy of this old-time apothecary's brews.

GETTING THERE

Located at the three-way intersection at 676 Charoen Krung Road
Tel 02-623-0718
Open 8.00–22.00 daily

SPECIALTY

Bitter medicine for a cough or sore throat (*yaa kom*); sweet medicine for a cold (*yaa waan*), 7 baht/glass, 25 baht/bottle
ยาขม สมุนไพรแก้ไอและเจ็บคอ และยาหวานแก้หวัด

NOTABLE EXTRAS

Tart-sweet flavor for excessive phlegm and as an anti-oxidant (*nam makham pom*), 7 baht/glass, 25 baht/ bottle; sweet, to strengthen the heart and for bruises (*nam bai bua bok*), 7 baht/glass, 25 baht/bottle; bittersweet, to balance the body (*nam geck huay*), 20 baht/bottle; sweet, to cool a heated body (*jab liang*), 20 baht/bottle

SEATING No

RESTROOM No

Best for
SNACKS

Lim Lao Ngo

ลิ้มเหล่าโหงว (ถนนทรงสวัสดิ์), ถนนทรงสวัสดิ์ หน้าบริษัทเจียไต๋

STREETSIDE CART, SONGSAWAD ROAD, CHINATOWN

At first glance, this unassuming mobile vendor in an outdoor food court might seem like no great deal but the packed tables attest otherwise. The prize is the super clear fish broth, acclaimed for its "unfishy" flavor.

GETTING THERE

From Songsawad Road, go into the road leading to Jiathai Co. (Songsawad Road) and you will find this vendor in the plaza in front, sharing space with a steamed dumpling cart
Open 19.00–23.00 daily

SPECIALTY
Noodles in fish broth with fish meatballs, 30 baht
ก๋วยเตี๋ยวน้ำ

OPTIONS
- Egg noodles (*bamee*), wide noodles (*sen yai*), thin noodles (*sen lek*)
- With broth (*nam*), without broth (*hang*), without noodles (*gow low*)

NOTABLE EXTRAS
Deep-fried fish skins, 15 baht/pack

SEATING Yes

ON THE TABLE
Chopsticks and Chinese spoons, fish sauce, vinegar with chilies, chili powder, white pepper

BEVERAGES
Chinese-style black iced coffee (*olieng*), black iced tea (*cha dum yen*), soft drink/carbonated beverage (*nam atlom*), red/green soda (*nam dang, nam kiew*), 12 baht; iced coffee (*gafae yen*), iced milk tea (*cha yen*), iced Milo (*Milo yen*), 15 baht; iced tea with lime, 20 baht; lime juice (*nam manao*), orange juice (*nam som*), 25 baht

RESTROOM No

Best for
FISH BALL NOODLES

Sieng Gi

เชี่ยงกี่ข้าวต้มปลา, ตรอกม้าเก็ง หลังโรงแรมแกรนด์ไชน่าปริ๊นเซส

SHOPHOUSE, TROK MA GENG, CHINATOWN

The price tag might seem a bit steep for a bowl of watery rice
with seafood at this hole-in-the-wall run by a husband and wife
team but the fish is tip-top fresh and there is a lot of it.
Bring a raging appetite, a couple of friends, or both.

GETTING THERE

On the left-hand side of Trok
Ma Geng behind the Grand
China Princess Hotel
Open 17.00–23.00 daily

Best for
**FISH
PORRIDGE**

SPECIALTY
Rice porridge with seabass,
pomfret or oysters, 200–300
baht (depending on size)

NOTABLE EXTRAS
Fish eggs on a bed of Chinese
celery, 200–300 baht (depending on size)
ข้าวต้มปลา กับปลากะพง
ปลาจาระเม็ด
หรือหอยนางรม

STANDARD TOPPINGS
Chinese celery, deep-fried
garlic, pickled cabbage

BEVERAGES
Cold tea water (*nam cha yen*),
free; bottled water, orange
juice (*nam som*), soft drink/
carbonated beverage (*nam
atlom*), 10 baht

SEATING Yes

ON THE TABLE
Tissues, toothpicks, fish sauce,
white vinegar with peppers,
ground white pepper

RESTROOM No

Samosa

ซาโมซา, ปากซอยห้างอินเดียเอ็มโพเรียม ถนนจักรเพชร

STREETSIDE CART, ENTRANCE TO SOI INDIA EMPORIUM, PAHURAT

Located in Little India (also known as Pahurat) right next to Chinatown, this cart offers an elegantly different savory snack option: freshly fried samosas and *tikki*, which resemble American crab cakes but are spicier than their samosa counterparts.

GETTING THERE

Direct your tuk-tuk to India Emporium in Pahurat. The samosa cart is located directly to the left of the building as you are facing it, at the entrance to a small lane **Tel** 02-222-0090, 087-684-1060, 087-811-2324
Open 9.00–18.30 Monday to Saturday, 10.00–18.30 Sunday

SPECIALTY
Samosas (Indian deep-fried dumplings stuffed with potatoes), 10 baht each

NOTABLE EXTRAS
Tikki (Indian soft breaded deep-fried patties stuffed with potatoes), 10 baht each

BEVERAGES No

SEATING No

RESTROOM No

Best for **SNACKS**

41

Banglamphu

This part of Bangkok, noted for its temples, old buildings and popularity with backpackers, is one of my favorite neighborhoods. Not only does it feature some great Thai street food but it also has plenty of other attractions, making a visit to the area a priority for most tourists.

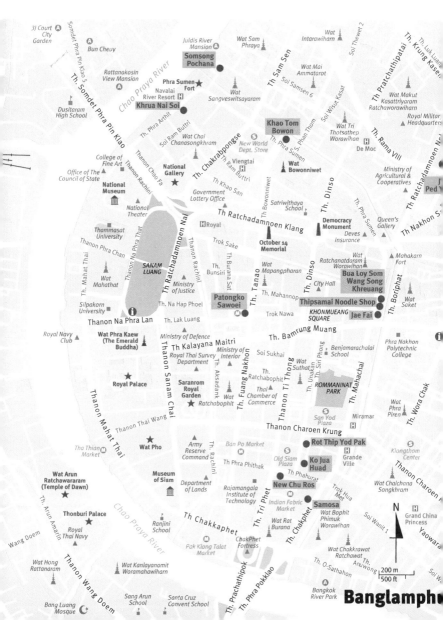

Khao Tom Bowon

ข้าวต้มบวร, ถนนพระสุเมรุ ตรงข้ามวัดบวรนิเวศน์ฯ

SHOPHOUSE, PHRA SUMEN ROAD, BANGLAMPHU

This old-fashioned Chinese-style rice porridge stand has grown over the past six decades from a small smattering of tables to a full-fledged restaurant with about 50 tables, including an air-conditioned room.

GETTING THERE

Located on Phra Sumen Road, under a green awning across the street from Bowonniwet Temple
Tel 02-629-1739
Open 15.00–3.00 except the last Tuesday of each month

SPECIALTY

Plain Thai-style rice porridge (*khao thom grub*) with a selection of side dishes, 5–10 baht a bowl (depending on size), 20–200 baht for sides
ข้ามต้ม และอาหารตามสั่ง

OPTIONS

- Rice porridge (*khao thom*), plain rice (*khao plow*)
- Sides range from pickled cabbage, 30 baht, to two deep-fried sea bass, 200 baht

SEATING Yes

ON THE TABLE

Chopsticks, Chinese spoons, tissues, bottled water

BEVERAGES

Fresh water (*nam plao*), 10 baht; soft drink/carbonated beverage (*nam atlom*), 15 baht; ice brought in trolley when you are seated

RESTROOM

Two squat toilets, no paper

Best for
RICE PORRIDGE

Bua Loy Som Wang Song Khreuang

บัวลอยสมหวังทรงเครื่อง, 315/1 ถนนมหาไชย ข้ามปั๊มน้ำมัน

STREETSIDE CART, 315/1 MAHACHAI ROAD, BANGLAMPHU

Just down the road from excellent *pad thai* and *lard na* (rice noodles in gravy) shops, this dessert stand is perfect for those still nursing a yen for something sweet. For something different, try the egg option.

GETTING THERE

Located at a mobile cart on Mahachai Road, next to the gas station
Tel 089-226-4382, 02-621-0082
Open 17.00–until they run out, except every other Monday

SPECIALTY
Sticky rice flour dumplings, taro and corn in warm coconut milk, 25–30 baht
บัวลอยเผือก มะพร้าว ข้าวโพด

OPTIONS
Without egg (*song khreuang*), 25 baht; with egg (*kai waan*), 30 baht; with egg white (*kai khao*), 30 baht; with salted egg (*kai kem*), 35 baht

SEATING Yes

ON THE TABLE
Nothing

BEVERAGES No

RESTROOM No

This dessert is delicious with or without the egg!

Best for DESSERTS

44

Patongko Sawoei

ปาท่องโก๋เสวย, ถนนตะนาว ตรงสี่แยกคอกวัว

STREETSIDE TAKEAWAY SHOP, TANAO ROAD, BANGLAMPHU

The no-nonsense owner of this stand is constantly kept busy frying up mounds of puffy, glistening, deep-fried *patongko*, known as "Chinese fried dough" or "the Emperor's bones". Freshly made, these *patongko* are admired by no less than the occupants of the royal palace.

GETTING THERE

On Tanao Road, located at Kokwiew intersection right after Prangputhorn Road
Tel 02-222-2635
Open 6.00–9.30, 16.30–21.00 daily

SPECIALTY
Deep-fried Chinese crullers (*patongko*) served Thai-style with a side of green-colored custard, 25 baht (small set), 40 baht (large set)
ปาท่องโก๋

NOTABLE EXTRAS
Deep-fried sweet Chinese buns (*salapao tod*), 4 baht each

SEATING No

BEVERAGES No

RESTROOM No

45

Khrua Nai Soi

ครัวในซอย, 100/2–3 ถนนพระอาทิตย์ ใกล้บ้านพระอาทิตย์

SHOPHOUSE, 100/2–3 PHRA ARTHIT ROAD, BANGLAMPHU

This bustling noodle spot specializing in beef broth thickened
with cow's blood (*nam tok*) caters mostly to the lunchtime crowd.
The deliciously thick meaty broth and the handmade pepper-vinegar sauce
flavoring it are the main draws here.

GETTING THERE

Located directly on 100/2–3 Phra
Arthit Road, a few steps down from
Baan Pra Arthit
Tel 086-982-9042
Open 7.00–18.00 except
the second and fourth
Wednesday of every month

Best for
BEEF NOODLE SOUP

SPECIALTY

Beef noodles with broth thickened with blood (*nam tok*),
50 baht (normal), 60 baht
(special, with more noodles)
ก๋วยเตี๋ยวเนื้อน้ำตก

OPTIONS

- Braised beef (*thun*), fresh
  beef (*sot*), beef meatballs
  (*luk chin*), entrails (*krueang
  nai*), tendon (*en*), mixed
  beef
- Rice vermicelli (*sen mee*),
  thin noodles (*sen lek*), wide

noodles (*sen yai*), without
noodles (*gow low*)
- With broth (*nam*), without
  broth (*hang*), without
  noodles (*gow low*), broth
  separate (*nam yaek*)

SEATING Yes

ON THE TABLE

Chopsticks and spoons,
tissues, condiment tray

BEVERAGES

Hot/cold coffee (*gafae ron/
yen*), hot/cold tea (*cha ron/
yen*), iced lemon tea (*cha

manao*), hot/cold cocoa
(*cocoa ron/yen*), hot/cold
Ovaltine (*Ovaltine ron/yen*),
limeade, pickled plum
juice (*nam buai*), 20 baht;
Chinese-style black iced
coffee (*olieng*), iced milk
(*nom yen*), 15 baht; soft
drink/carbonated beverage
(*nam atlom*), 10 baht;
Singha beer, 70 baht; Beer
Lao, 50 baht; fresh water
(*nam plao*), 2 baht

RESTROOM

Two urinals, one squat toilet,
no paper

Rot Thip Yod Pak (Baan Mo)

รสทิพย์ยอดผัก, บ้านหม้อ

SHOPHOUSE, BAAN MOR, BANGLAMPHU

Tucked away in a maze of stores selling electrical equipment, this unassuming shophouse serves up great red pork and gravy on rice and crispy angel hair noodles in gravy at reasonable prices. Stop by for a hearty lunch and then shop for household odds and ends on your way home.

GETTING THERE

From Old Siam shopping center at the McDonald's exit, cut across Baan Mor and make a left at the street 50 meters on your left
Tel 02-223-4562, 02-623-8475
Open 8.30–17.00 daily

Best for
PORK RICE

SPECIALTY
Rice topped with red pork (*khao moo dang*), 35 baht (regular), 45 baht (bigger serving); fried noodles in gravy with Chinese kale and pork (*lard na moo*), 35–45 baht (depending on size)
ข้าวหมูแดง

OPTIONS
- Pork rice: crispy pork rice (*khao moo krob*)
- Fried noodles in gravy: wide noodles (*sen yai*), rice vermicelli (*sen mee*), with egg (*sai kai*), soft (*nim*) or crispy (*mee krob*)

NOTABLE EXTRAS
Stir-fried noodles in soy sauce with or without egg (*pad see ew*), 40 baht

SEATING Yes

ON THE TABLE
Forks and spoons, toothpicks, jug of fresh water, black sweet soy sauce, red chili fish sauce, vinegar, chili powder, white pepper, scallions, sugar

BEVERAGES
Chinese-style black iced coffee (*olieng*), iced coffee (*gafae yen*), black iced tea (*cha dum yen*), iced milk tea (*cha yen*), 15 baht; soft drink/carbonated beverage (*nam atlom*), 12 baht

RESTROOM
Squat toilet, no paper

Jae Fai

เจ๊ไฝ, 327 ถนนมหาไชย ข้างๆ ร้านทิพย์สมัย

SHOPHOUSE, 327 MAHACHAI ROAD, BANGLAMPHU

The *Bangkok Post* has rhapsodized over Jae Fai, labeling the owner a "Mozart of the frying pan". They may be right. Her stall by the same name is known as not only having some of the best fried noodles in the city but as being one of Bangkok's best Thai dining spots, indoors or out.

GETTING THERE

Next to Thipsamai Noodle Shop on Mahachai Road
Tel 02-223-9384
Open 15.00–2.00 except Saturday

SPECIALTY

Noodles in gravy with seafood or shrimp, crispy or soft, from 360 baht (depending on size and substitutions)
ก๋วยเตี๋ยวราดหน้า
ทะเลหรือกุ้ง
เส้นกรอบหรือเส้นนุ่ม

OPTIONS

- With pork instead of seafood or shrimp (*moo*),

with chicken (*gai*), with or without egg (*sai kai, mai sai kai*), with extra vegetables (*pak perm*)
- Rice vermicelli (*sen mee*), wide noodles (*sen yai*)
- Soft traditional style (*nim*) or crispy (*grob*)

NOTABLE EXTRAS

Drunken spicy noodles with seafood or shrimp (*pad kee mow*), from 360 baht; stir-fried noodles with shrimp or seafood and egg (*guaythiew kua goong, talay*), from 360 baht; dry sukiyaki with shrimp or seafood (*suki hang goong, talay*), from 360 baht; dry congee (*jok hang*), from 360 baht; crab omelet (*kai jiew pu*), 800 baht

SEATING Yes

ON THE TABLE

Tissues, toothpicks, fish sauce, sugar, vinegar, chili powder, white pepper

BEVERAGES

Orange juice (*nam som*), 60 baht; coconut juice (*nam maphrao*), 50 baht; iced chrysanthemum tea (*geck huay yen*), longan juice (*nam lamyai*), 30 baht; soft drink/carbonated beverage (*nam atlom*), fresh water (*nam plao*), 12 baht; Singha beer, 110 baht; Heineken beer, 130 baht

RESTROOM

Squat toilet, no paper

Best for
FRIED NOODLES

Tom Yum Soup

inspired by Jae Fai

Jae Fai is quite rightly celebrated as one of the best street food cooks in Bangkok. While her fried noodle dishes are usually the ones to snag all the plaudits, it's her (surprisingly pricey 1,500 baht) spicy lemongrass soup studded with herbs, aromatics and gargantuan prawns that keeps me coming back.

4 servings

You will need

6 jumbo prawns with heads, deveined
5 cups water
1 heaped tsp roasted chili paste
6 large slices galangal
5–7 kaffir lime leaves (it's a lot, but if you are cooking in the spirit of Jae Fai, you will want this soup to "go up to 11"— her personal motto)
4 lemongrass bulbs (purple part), bruised
4–8 red chilies, bruised (this depends on your heat tolerance)
5 tbs fish sauce
1 shallot, sliced
1 cup mushrooms (I used oyster but straw or button mushrooms are fine)
1 cup young coconut shoots (if you can't find these, you might want to use something else that is tender yet crunchy, like peeled white asparagus)
juice of 2 limes

To make

1 Bring the water to the boil. Stir in the roasted chili paste.
2 Add the galangal, kaffir lime leaves, lemongrass and chilies. Allow to infuse for about 5 minutes, then bring to a simmer.
3 Add the shrimp heads, first scraping their contents into the soup. Wait 5 minutes, then season with the fish sauce. Add the mushrooms and coconut shoots.
4 Wait half an hour or until the shoots are tender. Skim the gunk off of the surface and discard the shrimp heads.
5 Turn off the heat, then add the cleaned shrimp and stir to turn the shrimp pink. Season with lime juice. Taste and adjust the seasoning accordingly.
6 Serve immediately, paired with rice and a Thai-style omelet, or in small individual bowls.

New Chu Ros

นิวชูรสโภชนา, 69–71 ซอยจินดามณี ในตลาดพาหุรัด

SHOPHOUSE, 69–71 SOI JINDAMANEE, PAHURAT MARKET, BANGLAMPHU

This bustling noodle shop looks incongruous amid the bolts of fabric and hanging *muumuus* in this outdoor market, which bridges the border between Chinatown and Pahurat (Little India). The pork noodles in broth and the pink seafood noodles are the biggest draws here.

GETTING THERE

Cross the road from the KFC in Old Siam and take the first alleyway (called Pahurat Market) to your left. New Chu Ros will be on your left about 100 meters along the alley
Tel 081-564-5663
Open 11.00–16.30 daily

NOTABLE EXTRAS

Coconut ice cream with various toppings, 15 baht

SEATING Yes

ON THE TABLE

Jug of fresh water, condiment tray, fish sauce, chili vinegar

BEVERAGES

Chinese-style black iced coffee (*olieng*), iced coffee (*gafae yen*), black iced tea (*cha dum yen*), iced milk tea (*cha yen*), 15 baht

RESTROOM

Squat toilet, no paper

SPECIALTY

Pork noodles in broth (*guaythiew moo*); red fermented tofu noodles (*yen ta fo*), 50 baht (regular), 60 baht (special)
ก๋วยเตี๋ยวหมู เย็นตาโฟ

Best for SOUP NOODLES

OPTIONS

- Pork (*moo*), red fermented tofu noodles (*yen ta fo*), fish (*krueang pla*), tart-spicy seasoning (*tom yum*)
- Wide noodles (*sen yai*), thin noodles (*sen lek*), rice vermicelli (*sen mee*), egg noodles (*bamee*), dumplings (*giew*), hand-rolled Chinese noodles (*giem ee*), glass vermicelli (*wunsen*), green hand-rolled noodles (*sieng hai*), without noodles (*gow low*)
- With broth (*nam*), without broth (*hang*), without noodles (*gow low*), broth separate (*nam yaek*)

Somsong Pochana

สมทรงโภชนา, ซอยวัดสังเวชฯ ข้ามสะพานข้างป้อมพระสุเมรุ อยู่ในซอยแรกทางซ้าย
หลังข้ามคลองแสนแสบ

SHOPHOUSE, SOI WAT SANGWACH, BANGLAMPHU

This noodle stand, with its buzzing clientele, big menu and
greedy pet cat who will not hesitate to bat your head for food, is like a
cross between a curry rice restaurant and someone's backyard.
The Sukhothai-style noodles are the stars of the show.

GETTING THERE

From Phra Arthit Road, take the
alleyway next to the Phra Sumen
fort, follow the bridge over Saen
Saeb Canal and then make a left
at the first alleyway on your left.
Somsong Pochana will be on your
right
Tel 02-282-0972
Open 9.30–16.00 daily

SPECIALTY
Sukhothai noodles (noodles
with pork slices, julienned
green beans and *pad Thai*-
style spices), 30 baht
ก๋วยเตี๋ยวสุโขทัย

OPTIONS
- Without pork (*mai sai moo*)
- Thin noodles (*sen lek*), wide
  noodles (*sen yai*), egg noodles (*bamee*), glass vermicelli (*wunsen*), hand-rolled
  Chinese noodles (*giem ee*)
- With broth (*nam*), without
  broth (*hang*), without
  noodles (*gow low*), broth
  separate (*nam yaek*)

NOTABLE EXTRAS
Rice with curry (*khao gub
gaeng*, selection changes
daily): one curry, 35 baht;
two types of curry, 40–50
baht (depending on type);
fermented rice noodles with

Best for
SOUP NOODLES

sweet coconut milk and
pineapple sauce (*khanom
jeen saonang*), 40 baht;
sticky rice dessert scented
with pandanus leaf and
served in hot coconut milk
(*khao fang*), 25 baht

SEATING Yes

ON THE TABLE
Tissues, jug of fresh water,
condiment tray

BEVERAGES
Iced coffee (*gafae yen*), black
iced tea (*cha dum yen*), iced
tea with lime, iced milk tea
(*cha yen*), 15 baht

RESTROOM
Western toilet, no paper

Thipsamai Noodle Shop

ผัดไทยทิพย์สมัย, 313 ถนนมหาไชย ตรงข้ามวัดราชนัดดา

SHOPHOUSE, 313 MAHACHAI ROAD, BANGLAMPHU

The most famous *pad Thai* spot in Bangkok has changed greatly since its humble beginnings as a tiny food stall but boasts the same laid-back ambiance and quick-fire service that turned it into the go-to place for in-the-know diners.

GETTING THERE

On Mahachai Road, across from the Raj Nad Da Temple. It is also known among taxi drivers as *pad Thai pratu pii* (pad Thai at the Ghost Gate)
Tel 02-221-6280
Open 17.00–3.00 daily

Best for PAD THAI

SPECIALTY

Pad Thai with fresh shrimp (*pad Thai goong sot*); "superb" *pad Thai* (*pad Thai piset*), 70 baht
ผัดไทยกุ้งสด และผัด
ไทยพิเศษ

OPTIONS

- With shrimp, without noodles, 70 baht
- Vegetarian, 40 baht
- "Deconstructed" *pad Thai* with bigger portions of shrimp and/or crabmeat (*pad Thai song kruenag*), 200 baht

SEATING Yes

ON THE TABLE

Tissues, fish sauce, dried chili powder, ground peanuts, vinegar with yellow peppers, sugar

BEVERAGES

Coconut shake, 15 baht; orange juice (*nam som*), big bottle, 90 baht; soft drink/ carbonated beverage (*nam atlom*), 8 baht (15 oz) or 7 baht (10 oz); fresh water (*nam plao*), 8 baht; black iced tea (*cha dum yen*), 2 baht

RESTROOM

Two squat toilets, no paper

Pad Thai

inspired by Thipsamai Noodle Shop

Thipsamai is one of the most popular, if not *the* most popular, *pad Thai* places in the country. The secret to its success lies in the deft, quick stir-frying of Thipsamai's many cooks, who spend the good part of every evening slaving over volcanically hot woks. However, the ingredients in Thipsamai's signature tart-sweet sauce are a secret. The sauce for this particular recipe is adapted from Chef McDang's *pad Thai* sauce in *The Principles of Thai Cookery*.

4 servings

You will need

1 liter water
1 cup chili sauce (I use ½ cup regular Sriracha and ½ cup Thai Sriracha, which is sweeter than the type used in the West)
180 ml white vinegar
¼ cup fish sauce
1 cup tamarind juice
1 tbs salt
¾ disc palm sugar
3 bird's eye chilies, sliced
150 g pickled garlic, plus all the pickled garlic juice from 1 container
4 tbs vegetable oil (for frying)
4 cloves garlic, minced
250 g shrimp, cleaned
100 g firm tofu, diced
4 tbs dried shrimp
250 g thin dried rice noodles, soaked in water
100 g Chinese pickled turnip
2 eggs
5 tbs roasted peanuts, ground (for garnish)
2 garlic chives, cut into 1 inch pieces (for garnish)
100 g bean sprouts, washed (for garnish)
1 lime, cut into wedges (for garnish)
½ banana blossom, cut into wedges (for garnish)
chili powder, sugar and fish sauce (for garnish)

To make

1 To make the *pad Thai* sauce, mix the water, chili sauce, vinegar, fish sauce, tamarind juice, salt, palm sugar, chilies, pickled garlic and its juice in a food processor or blender until smooth.
2 Bring the mixture to the boil in a saucepan, then simmer until the sauce thickens. Take off the heat.
3 In a wok, fry the garlic until fragrant and add the shrimp. Stir-fry until pink, remove and set aside.
4 Stir-fry the tofu with the dried shrimp until brown. Add the noodles and fry until soft, then add the *pad Thai* sauce gradually until it is soaked up by the noodles.
5 Add the pickled turnip.
6 In a separate bowl, crack the eggs and mix with a fork. Add to the wok gradually, along with the fried garlic and shrimp. Toss together.
7 Serve on a plate alongside the garnishes.

Jib Gi Ped Yang

จิ๊บกี่ เป็ดย่าง, ถนนนครสวรรค์ ตรงข้ามทางเข้าตลาดนางเลิ้ง

SHOPHOUSE, NAKHON SAWAN ROAD, BANGLAMPHU

Popular at lunchtime, this Thai-Chinese eatery has been around for decades, serving customers succulent, bone-free duck and satisfyingly crispy pork across the street from a bustling old-style wet market.

GETTING THERE

On Nakhon Sawan Road, across from Nang Lerng Market entrance
Tel 02-281-1283
Open 9.00–13.00 daily

SPECIALTY

Rice topped with grilled duck or red barbecued pork, 30–50 baht (depending on size)
ข้าวหน้าเป็ดหรือหมูแดง

NOTABLE EXTRAS

Stewed duck broth, 20 baht; duck innards, 30 baht; red or crispy pork, alone, 30–60 baht; grilled duck, alone, 85–170 baht; whole grilled duck, 340 baht; whole serving of grilled pork, 320 baht; bowl of rice, 7 baht

SEATING Yes

ON THE TABLE

Chopsticks, tissues, toothpicks, white pepper

BEVERAGES

Soft drink/carbonated beverage (*nam atlom*), 8 baht; beer, 70–80 baht

RESTROOM

Two squat toilets, no paper

Best for RED PORK/ DUCK RICE

Ko Jua Huad

โค้วจั๊วฮวด, 109 ถนนบูรพา ตรงข้ามศูนย์การค้าดิโอลด์สยาม

SHOPHOUSE, 109 BURAPHA ROAD, BANGLAMPHU

This open-air shophouse specializes in a particularly caloric treat: braised ham hock on rice. The dining area is packed at lunchtime, so try to arrive early to avoid sharing a table. Most patrons favor the fatty pork leg-topped rice and leave the calorie counting for another day.

GETTING THERE

Situated on the road that forms a perimeter around Old Siam, one of Bangkok's oldest shopping centers
Tel 084-163-6814, 081-933-4420
Open 8.00–15.30 except Sunday

SPECIALTY

Rice topped with braised pork leg (*khao ka moo*) or rice topped with extra fatty braised pork leg (*khao ka gi*), 50 baht; with hard-boiled egg (*sai kai*), 60 baht
ข้าวขาหมู ข้าวคากิ

OPTIONS

With hard-boiled egg (*sai kai*), without hard-boiled egg (*mai sai kai*)

NOTABLE EXTRAS

Rice topped with goose (*khao na haan*), 60–100 baht (depending on size of rice); topped with duck (*khao na ped*), 50 baht; noodles with duck, with or without broth (*guaythiew ped*), 50–60 baht; noodles with goose, with or without broth (*guaythiew haan*), 60–100 baht

SEATING Yes

ON THE TABLE

Jug of fresh water, fish sauce with chilies, sugar, chili powder, plain fish sauce, Golden Mountain sauce, fresh chilies, chili-studded vinegar, white pepper

BEVERAGES

Chinese-style black iced coffee (*olieng*), black iced tea (*cha dum yen*), 20 baht; iced coffee (*gafae yen*), iced milk tea (*cha yen*), 25 baht

RESTROOM

Squat toilet, no paper

Best for
PORK LEG RICE

Hualamphong (SAM YAN)

Four areas feature some of the best street food to be had in the city: around Hualamphong Train Station, home to a famous egg noodle vendor; around Traimit Temple where there is a smattering of well-loved vendors; the Sam Yan wet market; and the culinarily rich area known as Suan Luang Market, a section of town owned by Chulalongkorn University and thus heavily populated by university students on the lookout for tasty but cheap food.

Despite the area's popularity with university students, it is also known as a hidden paradise for Bangkok gourmets. Among the coffee spots and fast food chain restaurants lurk many food-related gems, both well-known and undiscovered. From streetside nibbles to desserts, from a Chinese-style rice porridge breakfast to a late night snack of fried noodles, the Hualamphong neighborhood is worth a visit for any Thai food lover.

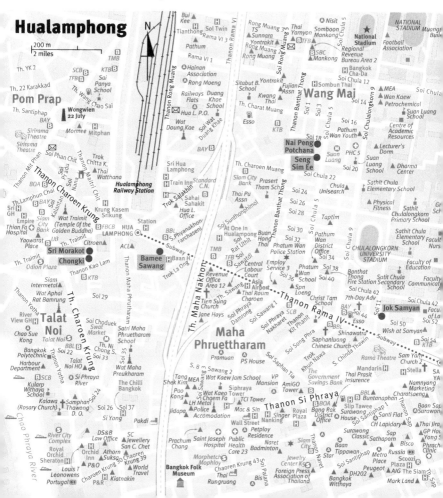

Bamee Sawang

สว่าง (หัวลำโพง) บะหมี่ปู, ถนนพระรามสี่ ฝั่งตรงข้ามสถานีรถไฟหัวลำโพง

SHOPHOUSE, RAMA IV ROAD, HUALAMPHONG

Distinctive for its fluorescent green lighting, this egg noodle stand has long enjoyed a reputation as one of the best places for a bowl of noodles, thanks to its buttery, rich strands. Just make sure not to bring in alcoholic drinks.

GETTING THERE

Located on Rama IV Road, across from the Hong Kong noodle shop and Hualamphong train station
Tel 02-236-1772, 081-618-1884
Open 17.00–23.00 except Monday and religious holidays

Best for **EGG NOODLES**

SPECIALTY

Egg noodles with shrimp wontons, barbecued pork and crabmeat, 50 baht; egg noodles with shrimp wontons, barbequed pork and crab claw, 150 baht
บะหมี่เกี๊ยวกุ้ง ปู หมูแดง,
บะหมี่เกี๊ยวก้ามปู หมูแดง

OPTIONS

- Egg noodles only (*bamee*), wontons only (*giew*), both (*mee giew*)
- Barbecued pork (*moo daeng*), crabmeat (*pu*), extra crispy pork (*moo grob*), crab claw (*gam pu*)
- With broth (*nam*), without broth (*hang*), without noodles (*gow low*), broth separate (*nam yaek*)

STANDARD TOPPINGS

Chopped scallions, pickled cabbage, deep-fried garlic

NOTABLE EXTRAS

Steamed shrimp dumplings (*khanom jeeb*), 100 baht

BEVERAGES

Chrysanthemum tea (*geck huay*), Chinese herbal beverage (*lorhangguay*), lime juice (*nam manao*); with ice, 10 baht, without ice, 20 baht, plain ice, 2 baht

SEATING Yes

ON THE TABLE

Framed newspaper and magazine commendations, jug of fresh water, condiment tray, Chinese black vinegar (*zisho*)

RESTROOM

Squat toilet, no paper

57

Chongki

ชองกี่ หมูสะเต๊ะ, 84–88 ซอยสุกร 1 หลังโชว์รูมยนตรกิจ

SHOPHOUSE, 84–88 SOI SUGORN 1, HUALAMPHONG

In the hotly contested realm of pork satays, Chongki has consistently remained among the best as the daily queue of idling cars awaiting pork satay pick-ups attests. Chongki also serves thick hunks of freshly grilled bread, delicious accompaniments to a hearty snack or simple meal.

GETTING THERE

Close to Wat Traimit along Soi Sugorn 1
Tel 081-615-8733, 081-656-2468, 02-233-4100, 02-236-1171, 02-639-6584
Open 9.30–19.30 daily

SPECIALTY
Pork or liver satay, 6.50 baht/stick, accompanied by peanut sauce and cucumber-shallot-chili salsa (*ajard*)
หมูหรือตับสะเต๊ะ

NOTABLE EXTRAS
Extra cucumbers for *salsa*, 10 baht; grilled bread, 8 baht a slice, 15 baht for two slices

SEATING Yes

ON THE TABLE
Tissues, toothpicks, jug of tea water, black soy sauce, vinegar with chilies

BEVERAGES
Chinese-style black iced coffee (*olieng*), roselle juice (*nam krajiep*), pickled plum juice (*nam buai*), soft drink/carbonated beverage (*nam atlom*), fresh water (*nam plao*), 10 baht

Best for
SNACKS

RESTROOM
Western toilet, bowl of water to flush, no paper

Sri Morakot

ข้าวหมูแดงสีมรกต, 80-82 ซอยสุกร 1 ถนนไตรมิตร ข้าง ๆ ร้านชองกี

SHOPHOUSE, 80–82 SOI SUGORN 1, HUALAMPHONG

Right next door to the pork satay institution Chongki, this barbecued pork stand attracts an even bigger crowd than its better known neighbor. Luckily for fans of both stands, customers can sit at either one and order from both.

GETTING THERE

Along Traimit Road, next to the Chongki pork satay stand
Tel 081-567-9006, 081-816-9774
Open 11.00–20.00 daily

SPECIALTY

Rice with barbecued pork, 35 baht (regular); special with barbecued and crispy pork, plus pork sausage, 70 baht
ข้าวหมูแดง

OPTIONS

- Barbecued pork (*moo daeng*), crispy pork (*moo grob*), mixed (special or *piset*)
- With hard-boiled egg (*kai*), 40 baht (regular), 77 baht (special)
- Without rice (*moo yang diew*), 80 baht (for three varieties of pork)

NOTABLE EXTRAS

Soup with stewed duck and pickled lime, soup with bitter melon and pork ribs, soup with pork stomach and pickled cabbage (*krapho moo*) (Sunday only), 25 baht

STANDARD TOPPINGS

Sliced cucumbers on the side

BEVERAGES

Chrysanthemum tea (*geck huay*), guava juice (*nam farang*), sugarcane juice (*nam tansot*), longan juice (*nam lamyai*), roselle juice (*nam krajiep*), pickled plum juice (*nam buai*), tamarind juice (*nam makham*), 12 baht

SEATING Yes

ON THE TABLE

Tissues, jug of tea water, fish sauce, sweet soy sauce, vinegar with chilies, green onions

RESTROOM

Two squat toilets, no paper

Best for
RICE
PORK

Nai Peng Potchana

นายเพ้ง ราชาก๋วยเตี๋ยวคั่วไก่, จุฬาซอย 18 ตลาดสวนหลวง

SHOPHOUSE, CHULA SOI 18, SAM YAN, HUALAMPHONG

**This smoke-filled, relatively spacious open-air dining area is popular
with students from nearby Chulalongkorn University. The specialty
here is tasty stir-fried noodles or processed squid strings
with plenty of chicken chunks or chicken and seafood.**

**Best for
FRIED
CHICKEN
NOODLES**

SPECIALTY
Stir-fried flat wide noodles with chicken, egg and seafood, 35 baht (regular), 40 baht (special portion)
ก๋วยเตี๋ยวคั่วไก่

OPTIONS
- Chicken (*gai*), seafood (*talay*), chicken and seafood (*gai talay*)
- Rice noodles (*guaythiew*), processed fish snack (*taro*)

STANDARD TOPPINGS
Shredded lettuce

BEVERAGES
Chinese-style black iced coffee (*olieng*), chrysanthemum tea (*geck huay*), longan juice (*nam lamyai*), roselle juice (*nam krajiep*), orange juice (*nam som*), 15 baht

SEATING Yes

ON THE TABLE
Toothpicks, jug of tea water, condiment tray with fish sauce, sweet chili sauce, chili powder, vinegar with peppers, sugar

RESTROOM
Western toilet, no paper

Jok Samyan

โจ๊กสามย่าน, จุฬาซอย 11 ริมถนนตรงข้ามร้านอาหารนครโภชนา

SHOPHOUSE, CHULA SOI 11, SAM YAN

A Bangkok street food institution, Jok Samyan has become synonymous with good Chinese-style rice porridge stirred slowly over a low flame so that the rice grains break down gradually into a smooth texture. Don't expect anything other than rice porridge from this no-frills menu.

GETTING THERE
Located in Chula Soi 11 on the side of the road opposite from the Nakorn Pochana restaurant
Tel 02-216-480
Open 5.00–9.00, 15.30–21.00 daily

SPECIALTY
Chinese-style rice porridge with bone-in pork pieces 35 baht (regular); 40 baht (with egg); 45 baht (special size); 50 baht (special size with egg)
โจ๊ก

OPTIONS
With egg (*sai kai*), no egg (*mai kai*), extra pork (*moo piset*), extra size (*piset*)

SEATING Yes

ON THE TABLE
Tissues, toothpicks, chili powder, sliced chilies in vinegar, Maggi sauce, white pepper, sugar, deep-fried dough squiggles (10 baht)

BEVERAGES
Bottled water, soft drink/carbonated beverage (*nam atlom*) 10 baht; tea water (*nam cha*), free

RESTROOM
Squat toilet, bowl of water to flush, no paper

Best for
PORK
RICE
PORRIDGE

Seng Sim Ee

เซ็งซิมอี้, ตลาดสวนหลวง ตรงข้ามที่จอดรถ

SHOPHOUSE, SUAN LUANG MARKET, SAM YAN

This stand specializes in shaved ice desserts (*nam khaeng sai*), ranging from *thao tung*, a mix of Chinese delicacies such as gingko nuts and black jelly in syrup, to Thai offerings like *selim*, a multi-colored sweet vermicelli or sweet melon chunks in coconut milk.

GETTING THERE

On the main road of Suan Luang Market, known as Thalad Suan Luang among taxi drivers, across from a parking lot
Tel 02-214-0612, 089-770-2618
Open 18.00–midnight daily

SPECIALTY

Selection of fruit, dumplings and jellies in syrup, longan juice or coconut milk, topped with shaved ice (*nam khaeng sai*), 20–40 baht (depending on selection)
น้ำแข็งใส

OPTIONS

- The "buffet" section in front offers a mind-blowing array of delicacies served with a mound of shaved ice on top, so let your imagination run wild
- Selections include the Chinese-inspired longan juice-based desserts (usually containing ingredients like gingko nuts, lotus root or mouse-ear mushrooms) and coconut-milk based ones (often paired with *tubtim grob*, red crunchy tapioca dumplings or fruit)

If you cannot decide, a "menu" inside offers suggestions, such as *tubtim grob*, melon and taro root in coconut milk

SEATING Yes

ON THE TABLE Tissues

RESTROOM Squat toilet, no paper

Best for **DESSERTS**

Silom/Sathorn

Although the Silom/Sathorn area is known as the heart of Bangkok's commercial district, it is not really renowned for its street food aside from a handful of well-known places. While it is easy to find a quick and easy spot for whatever type of food you desire, be it street food or more formal Asian or Western dining, this neighborhood does offer up some culinary treasures if you look hard enough. Brave the crowds and chaos and you are likely to be rewarded with both a good meal and, if you stay out late enough, an interesting look into Bangkok's nightlife.

Khao Mok Gai Convent

ข้าวหมกไก่ คอนแวนต์, ถนนคอนแวนต์ แยกถนนสีลม หน้าร้านอาหารบัว

STREETSIDE CART, CONVENT ROAD, SILOM

Delicious Thai-Muslim yellow rice flavored with fragrant "Islamic spices" (*krueng tet Islam*), crowned with a meaty chicken leg is the name of the game here. Don't order your rice without the accompanying spicy chicken soup.

GETTING THERE

A mobile cart in the daytime, Khao Mok Gai is located directly on Convent Road in front of Bua Restaurant
Tel 086-042-4645
Open 11.30–17.30 Monday to Friday

SPECIALTY

Thai-Muslim chicken with yellow rice, 35–55 baht (depending on size of portions); chicken soup, 30 baht
ข้าวหมกไก่

OPTIONS

Regular (*tamada*), 35 baht; extra rice (*piset khao*), 40 baht; extra chicken (*piset gai*), 50 baht; both extra (*tung khao gai*), 55 baht

SEATING Yes

ON THE TABLE

Jug of fresh water

BEVERAGES

Chinese-style black iced coffee (*olieng*), black iced tea (*cha dum yen*), Iced chrysan-themum tea (*geck huay yen*), 10 baht

RESTROOM No

Jay Ouan Moo Jum

เจ๊อ้วนหมูจุ่ม สวนพลู, ถนนสวนพลู ปากทางเข้าสวนพลูซอย 3

STREETSIDE CART, OUTSIDE ENTRANCE TO SUAN PLU SOI 3, SATHORN

This down-home Isaan joint features a wide range of dishes
you can tick off of their handy order sheet, including various
grated salads (*som tum*). But the real special here is *moo jum*,
a sort of sukiyaki-like brew that incorporates spicy and tart flavors.

GETTING THERE

Located to the right of the entrance
to Suan Plu Soi 3, the tables stretch
out along the sidewalk from the
main grill
Tel 086-170-5806
Open 17.00–2.00 daily

SPECIALTY
Moo jum, 180 baht
หมูจุ่ม

NOTABLE EXTRAS
Grilled fatty pig's neck
(*kho moo yang*), 70 baht

SEATING Yes

ON THE TABLE
Nothing. Ask for tissues
(a roll of toilet paper)

BEVERAGES
Heineken beer, 100 baht;
Leo beer, 80 baht; Singha
beer, 90 baht; Saengsom
whisky (small bottle), 240
baht; soft drink/carbonated
beverage (*nam atlom*), 15
baht, large bottle, 50 baht;
ice, 10 baht; bottled water,
15 baht; SPY cooler, 50 baht

RESTROOM No

Best for
ISAAN
DISHES

Recipe for
Squid Salad

inspired by Jay Ouan Moo Jum

While grilled pork collar is the star attraction at Jay Ouan Moo Jum, the *yum pla muk*, or spicy squid salad, has proven almost as popular. Flavorful and full of different textures, it is also very easy to make. Adjust the dressing to suit your taste.

4 servings

You will need

2 squid, gutted, cleaned and sliced
½ yellow onion, sliced
2 stalks Thai celery, sliced (or 1 stalk Western celery, sliced)
6 bird's eye chilies, sliced
1 tomato, sliced
3–4 tbs fish sauce
juice of 1 lime
1 tsp sugar (or to taste)

To make

1 Blanch the squid in boiling water for a minute, taking care not to overcook it. The squid will be cooked before you expect it.
2 Put the squid in a bowl and add the sliced onion, celery, bird's eye chilies and tomato.
3 Mix the fish sauce, lime juice and sugar and taste. Adjust the seasoning as you see fit. Pour over the ingredients in the bowl.
4 Allow the flavors to meld for a few minutes. Serve at room temperature.

JC Yen Ta Fo

เย็นตาโฟ เจ.ซี., ศาลาแดงซอย 2 สุดซอย ใกล้ถนนคอนแวนต์

STREETSIDE CART, SALADAENG SOI 2, CLOSE TO CONVENT ROAD

**The no-nonsense owner may rub some patrons up the wrong way,
but if you are willing to look past his brusque manner
you will find a generously sized portion of delicious
pink sauce noodles with no need for extra seasonings.**

GETTING THERE

Across from a dorm for Bangkok Christian College, near the intersection of Saladaeng Soi 2 and Convent Road
Tel 081-814-9547, 081-919-1233
Open 6.00–9.20, 10.00–13.30 except Sunday

Best for **NOODLE SOUP**

SPECIALTY
Red fermented tofu noodles (*yen ta fo*), 40 baht (regular), 45 baht (special size)
เย็นตาโฟ

OPTIONS
- Wide noodles (*sen yai*), thin noodles (*sen lek*), rice vermicelli (*sen mee*)
- With broth (*nam*), without broth (*hang*), without noodles (*gow low*), broth separate (*nam yaek*)

SEATING Yes

ON THE TABLE
Chopsticks and Chinese spoons, bottled water, condiment tray, chili powder

BEVERAGES
Coke or green Fanta, 5 baht a glass; small bottle of water, 3 baht; big bottle of water, 5 baht; extra ice, 2 baht

RESTROOM No

Kho Moo Yang

inspired by Jay Ouan Moo Jum

This recipe, inspired by the sticky, sweet, lacquered fatty pork specimens found on the grill at Bangkok Isaan-style standby, Jay Ouan Moo Jum (p. 66), was difficult to come by but easy to do. You can increase the ratio of sweet soy sauce to soy sauce to make this even sweeter, but the coriander roots are what really makes this recipe Thai.

3–4 servings

You will need

400 g pork collar (or shoulder)
4 garlic cloves
2–3 coriander roots, washed
½ tsp white peppercorns
¼ cup soy sauce
1 tbs sweet soy sauce
1 tbs brown sugar

Method

1 Pound the garlic, coriander roots and peppercorns into a paste in a mortar and pestle. Add the soy sauce and sweet soy sauce and mix with the spices to form a marinade. Add the brown sugar.

2 In a large mixing bowl, pour the marinade over the pork and leave for at least four hours, preferably overnight.
3 Grill the meat until brown and charred a little at the edges. If you don't own a grill, heat up a heavy pan (cast-iron, preferably) that has been oiled beforehand and brown the pork until it is a nice caramel color. Then put the pork and pan into the oven that has been set at 180 degrees Celsius for about 15 minutes or until the edges of the pork gain the same charred edges and sticky-looking exterior that you would have gotten via grilling.
4 Slice the pork and serve with a tamarind or sweet chili sauce, along with some sticky rice.

Polo Fried Chicken

ไก่ทอดเจ๊กี (โปโล), 137/1–2 ซอยโปโล แยกถนนวิทยุ

SHOPHOUSE, 137/1–2 SOI POLO, WIRELESS ROAD

This long-standing fried chicken spot has morphed from its humble streetside origins into a bona fide restaurant. All the same, no street food guide is complete without this stalwart. Despite recent renovations, the focus remains on the simplicity of Isaan food.

GETTING THERE

Known as Soi Polo among taxi drivers, Soi Sanam Klee features Polo Fried Chicken on its left-hand side and is almost impossible to miss
Tel 02-655-8489, 081-300-4444
Open 7.00–22.00 daily

SPECIALTY

Fried chicken (*gai tod*), 200 baht for a whole bird; green papaya salad (*somtum Thai*), 40 baht; sticky rice (*khao niew*), 15 baht
ไก่ทอด ส้มตำ ข้าวเหนียว

NOTABLE EXTRAS

Shredded bamboo shoot salad (*sup naw mai*), 40 baht; grilled pork shoulder (*kaw moo yang*), 60 baht; spicy Isaan-style soup (*tom sap*), 60–80 baht

SEATING Yes

ON THE TABLE

Bottled water, tissues, toothpicks, sweet chili dipping sauce, spicy *jaew* dipping sauce

BEVERAGES

Soft drink/carbonated beverage (*nam atlom*), 15–30

baht; fresh water (*nam plao*) and ice, 10 baht; plain carbonated water, 15 baht; beer, 60–90 baht

RESTROOM

Western toilet, relatively clean

Best for ISAAN DISHES

Sukhumvit

It may not seem like it, but tucked in among the Japanese restaurants, wine bars and cafés are some great vendors offering serious street food. You just have to know where to look. Individual vendors ply their trade from well-worn shophouses, open either early in the morning or late at night after the clubs close, and everyone, from motorcycle taxi drivers to sloshed Bangkok club-goers, is happy to partake of a quick noodle snack on the go.

Sukhumvit is also home to one of Bangkok's best-known informal food centers, referred to among locals as "Soi 38". A collection of different vendors massed at the entrance to Sukhumvit Soi 38 and open generally from 6 pm onward, Soi 38 offers the ideal opportunity for street food beginners to dip a toe into the world of Thai street food. Almost all the stalls located here are hygienic and offer first-rate food. Even better, diners can sample the offerings of multiple food stalls at the convenience of one table.

Snagging and retaining a table means finding a vendor from whom you will order at least one dish. After that, the table is basically yours for the rest of the evening. After placing your orders with other vendors, simply tell them where you are seated and they will bring the food to you. You pay after you receive your food. The condiment trays are in high demand so try to flavor your dish as quickly as possible after you receive your order.

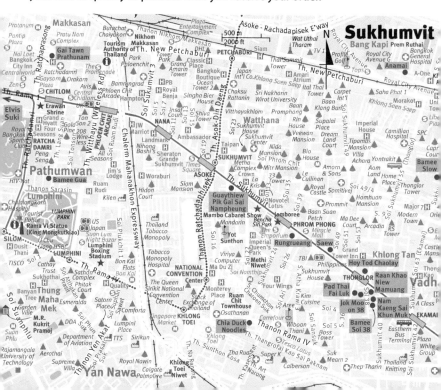

Hoy Tod Chaolay

หอยทอด ชาวเล, ถนนทองหล่อ ราว 50 เมตรจากปากซอย ฝั่งซ้าย

SHOPHOUSE, THONGLOR ROAD, SUKHUMVIT

Popular with Japanese expatriates, Hoy Tod Chaolay is patronized by *pad Thai* hungry diners who crave a ready plate of fried noodles but who don't want to trek all the way to the Old City.

GETTING THERE

Located near the entrance to Thonglor Road, about 50 meters on the left-hand side when coming from Sukhumvit Road
Tel 085-128-3996
Open 9.00–21.00 daily

SPECIALTY

Pad Thai with fresh shrimp (*pad thai goong sod*), 60 baht; with seafood (*pad thai talay*), 60 baht; oyster omelet (*hoy tod nangrom*), 60–80 baht
ผัดไทยใส่กุ้ง

OPTIONS

With glass vermicelli (*wunsen*), 40 baht; with dried shrimp, (*goong hang*), 40 baht

NOTABLE EXTRAS

Mussel omelet (*hoy tod mangpu*), 50 baht; Chinese-style fried oysters (*aw suan*), 60–80 baht; Chinese-style fried oysters with one side crispy (*aw luea*), 60–80 baht

STANDARD TOPPINGS

Side dishes of *thon guay chai* (a type of scallion), bean sprouts, lime wedges

BEVERAGES

Iced coffee (*gafae yen*), iced lemon tea (*cha manao*), chrysanthemum tea (*geck huay*), guava juice (*nam farang*), roselle juice (*nam krajiep*), soft drink/carbonated beverage (*nam atlom*), fresh water (*nam plao*), 15 baht; Singha beer, 75 baht; Heineken beer, 90 baht

SEATING Yes

ON THE TABLE

Tissues, toothpicks, bottled water, jugs of water, condiment tray (chili powder, sugar, ground peanuts), fish sauce, sweet chili sauce, vinegar with peppers

RESTROOM No

Best for
PAD THAI

Bamee Slow

บะหมี่สโลว์, ทางเข้าเอกมัยซอย 19

SHOPHOUSE, EKAMAI 19, SUKHUMVIT

Street food aficionados may be puzzled as to why the customers who throng this no-nonsense shophouse are willing to wait for up to 30 minutes for a single bowl. The answer is the tastiest Chinese-style egg noodles with soft-boiled egg (*bamee kai*) this side of Chinatown.

GETTING THERE

Located at the entrance to Ekamai Soi 19, on the left-hand side
Open 20.30–3.00 daily

Best for
EGG NOODLE SOUP

SPECIALTY

Chinese-style egg noodles with roasted pork and wonton dumplings, with pork broth, with minced pork served separately, 40 baht (for noodles), 15 baht (for broth)
บะหมี่หมูแดงและเกี๊ยว

OPTIONS

- Roasted pork (*moo daeng*), minced pork (*moo sab*), egg boiled in broth (*kai*), Chinese kale (*pak kiew*)
- Egg noodles (*bamee*), wonton dumplings (*giew*), thin noodles (*sen lek*), without noodles (*gow low*)
- With broth (*nam*), without broth (*hang*), without noodles (*gow low*), broth separate (*nam yaek*), spicy-tart (*tom yum*) (if ordering thin noodles)

STANDARD TOPPINGS

For egg noodles: scallions, coriander, pickled cabbage, crispy pork rinds. For *tom yum* noodles: peanuts, scallions, coriander, bean sprouts

BEVERAGES

Soft drinks, 10 baht; self-service metal cups and ice next to vending cart

SEATING Yes

ON THE TABLE

Chopsticks, tea water, condiments (sugar, fish sauce, vinegar, chili pepper)

RESTROOM No

Bamee Slow Egg Noodles

inspired by Bamee Slow

This is a stab at a serious street food favorite—egg noodles. If you have fresh egg noodles to hand, great. Just make sure to rinse off the excess flour before using. If you don't, instant ramen without the artificial seasonings can work at a pinch! Also make up each serving one by one as this really does make a difference.

4 servings

You will need

200 g pork soup bones
500 ml water
2 garlic cloves
5–10 white peppercorns, depending on taste
1 tsp *nam prik pow* (roasted chili paste)
1 tsp salt
3 tbs soy sauce
200 g minced pork
4 stalks Chinese broccoli or kale
200 g fresh egg noodles
2 eggs, soft-boiled (boiled for 3–4 minutes), cooled in an ice bath and peeled
sugar, chili powder, fish sauce, white vinegar (for garnish)

To make

1 Boil the pork bones, cloves and peppercorns for an hour, skimming the surface periodically.
2 Season with the roasted chili paste salt, salt and soy sauce, and more white pepper. Adjust to taste.

3 Add the minced pork and allow to boil for a few minutes until the pork is cooked, skimming the scum off of the surface.
4 Add the greens.
5 Place half of the noodles in a strainer and immerse in the broth, skimming more scum off the surface, if necessary. Wait 2–3 minutes for the noodles to cook and lose their starch.

6 Place the noodles in a bowl and ladle the broth with minced pork (but not the pork bones) over the noodles. Garnish with egg and greens and, if you have it, a few slices of Chinese-style barbecued red pork.
7 Serve alongside sugar, chili powder, fish sauce, white vinegar (with or without sliced or smashed chilies) and ground peanuts, if you like.

Pad Thai Fai Luk

ผัดไทยไฟลุก (สุขุมวิท 38), แยกแรกตรงปากซอยสุขุมวิทซอย 38

MOBILE VENDOR, SUKHUMVIT 38, SUKHUMVIT

This tiny cart is consistently mobbed for its award-winning *pad Thai*,
a well-seasoned mass of noodles with generous accompaniments.
The version here can be a little too sweet for more traditional taste buds.

GETTING THERE

At the end of the sub-soi on
Sukhumvit 38
Open 20.00–3.00 daily

SPECIALTY
Pad Thai with freshly fried
shrimp (50 baht)
ผัดไทยกุ้งสด

OPTIONS
With or without egg
covering (*haw kai*)

NOTABLE EXTRAS
Thai-Chinese oyster/egg
casserole (*aw suan*),
150 baht

STANDARD TOPPINGS
Raw banana blossom (*bai hua
plee*), a type of scallion (*thon
guay chai*), bean sprouts

BEVERAGES No

SEATING Yes

ON THE TABLE
Nothing (condiment tray
served along with noodles)

RESTROOM No

Best for PAD THAI

Jok Moo on 38

โจ๊กหมู (เจ้าเก่าทองหล่อ) สุขุมวิท 38,
ปากซอยสุขุมวิท 38 ตรงหัวมุมซอยแยก ฝั่งขวาของซอย

SHOPHOUSE, SUKHUMVIT 38, SUKHUMVIT

Porridge lovers flock to this rice porridge stand known for its hygiene and consistently good food. Seating is available in a "restaurant" behind the food cart but many come simply to take home porridge for breakfast.

GETTING THERE

At the entrance to Sukhumvit Soi 38, right after the entrance to the sub-soi, on the right-hand side of the street
Tel 02-381-1614
Open 16.00–midnight daily

SPECIALTY

Jok, or Chinese-style rice porridge with pork, 25–55 baht (depending on additions)
โจ๊ก

Best for RICE PORRIDGE

OPTIONS

- With pork (*moo*) only, with preserved salted egg (*kai kem*), with Chinese "century egg" (*kai yiew maa*)
- With egg (*sai kai*), without egg (*mai sai kai*)
- With innards (liver, small intestine, stomach, kidney) (*sai krueang nai*), without innards (*mai sai krueang nai*)
- Regular or special (bigger) size (*piset*)

STANDARD TOPPINGS

Sliced green onion, julienned ginger

BEVERAGES

Chrysanthemum tea (*geck huay*), lemongrass juice (*nam takrai*) roselle juice (*nam krajiep*), 15 baht; fresh water (*nam plao*), 10 baht

SEATING

On the sidewalk

ON THE TABLE

Toothpicks, bottled water, condiment tray,

RESTROOM

Bathroom in back, squat toilet, no paper

Nam Kaeng Sai Khun Muk

มุกเต้าทึงสุขุมวิท 38 (น้ำแข็งใสคุณมุก),
สุขุมวิทซอย 38 ราว 50 เมตรจากปากซอย ฝั่งซ้าย

STREETSIDE VENDOR, SUKHUMVIT 38, SUKHUMVIT

Let your imagination run riot at this old-style Thai dessert counter
where any combination of jellies, fruits or dumplings
can be combined with a number of different syrups and
served with shaved ice on top.

GETTING THERE

About 50 meters from the entrance
to Sukhumvit Soi 38, on the left
Tel 02-381-1614
Open 18.00–2.00 daily

Best for
DESSERTS

SPECIALTY

Mix of dumplings, jellies and
fruit served with a selection
of syrups and topped with
shaved ice (*nam khaeng sai*),
20 baht
น้ำแข็งใส

OPTIONS

- "Chinese-style" *thao tung*,
  with a mix of delicacies
  such as gingko nuts and
  lotus stem with longan
  juice (*nam lamyai*) or ginger broth (*nam king*) with
  shaved ice, or served hot
  with egg
- "Thai-style", with a mix of
  jellies or delicacies such
  as *selim*, a multi-colored
  vermicelli, with coconut
  milk and shaved ice
- Many combinations, mix
  and match to your heart's
  delight

NOTABLE EXTRAS

Dumplings in warm coconut
milk with sweet egg (*bua loy
kai waan*), 20 baht; coconut

ice cream, 20 baht; toast with
custard, 30 baht

BEVERAGES

Iced coffee (*gafae yen*), black
iced tea (*cha dum yen*), iced
milk tea (*cha yen*), 12 baht;
Pepsi, 10 baht

SEATING Yes

ON THE TABLE
Nothing

RESTROOM No

Raan Khao Niew Mamuang
(Nhungnhing)

ร้านข้าวเหนียวมะม่วง (หนุงหนิง) สุขุมวิท 38 ในซอยฝั่งขวา ติดกับแผงร้านขายน้ำ

MOBILE VENDOR, SUKHUMVIT 38, SUKHUMVIT

This open-air stall in front of Suthi Mansion on Sukhumvit Soi 38 may be the best mango sticky rice stand in the city. Perennially ripe mangoes—both *okkrong*, valued for its superior fragrance, and *nam dok mai*, which is juicy and less fibrous—are available.

GETTING THERE

Sukhumvit Soi 38, in the right-hand alleyway next to a drinks stand
Tel 086-655-2752
Open 18.00–3.00 daily

SPECIALTY
Mango with sticky rice (*khao niew mamuang*), 60 baht (small), 70 baht (medium), 80 baht (large)
ข้าวเหนียวมะม่วง

OPTIONS
Okkrong or *nam dok mai* mangoes

NOTABLE EXTRAS
Durian with sticky rice (*khao niew durian*), 50 baht

BEVERAGES No

SEATING Yes, shared with egg noodle and *pad Thai* vendors

ON THE TABLE
Nothing

RESTROOM No

Best for DESSERTS

Rungrueang

ก๋วยเตี๋ยวรุ่งเรือง, ปากซอยสุขุมวิท 26

SHOPHOUSE, SUKHUMVIT SOI 26, SUKHUMVIT

This noodle spot is so popular with the workday lunchtime crowd that it has its own parking lot across the street. It is actually a pair of adjacent shops run by the two sons of the founder, but both serve basically the same bowl of noodles with minced pork.

GETTING THERE

About 100 meters into Sukhumvit Soi 26, on the right-hand side, roughly across the street from the gas station
Tel 02-258-6744
Open 8.30–16.30 daily

SPECIALTY
Noodles with minced pork and *tom yum* (spicy-tart) broth, without broth but with *tom yum* seasonings, 40 baht (regular), 50 baht (special, bigger serving)
ก๋วยเตี๋ยวหมูต้มยำ
หรือแห้งต้มยำ

OPTIONS
- Minced pork, freshly boiled fish balls, deep-fried fish balls, innards or "standard" (all)
- Egg noodles (*bamee*), wide noodles (*sen yai*), thin noodles (*sen lek*), rice vermicelli (*sen mee*)
- With broth (*nam*), plain or *tom yum*, without broth (*hang*), plain or *yum* style, (topped with chili powder, chopped peanuts, green onion, coriander and bean sprouts), without noodles (*gow low*), broth separate (*nam yaek*)

STANDARD TOPPINGS
Deep-fried garlic, chopped green onions, bean sprouts

SIDES
Crispy fish skins (15 baht)

BEVERAGES
Chinese-style black iced coffee (*olieng*), black iced tea (*cha dum yen*), longan juice (*nam lamyai*), Coke, Sprite, fresh water (*nam plao*), 10 baht

SEATING Yes

ON THE TABLE
Chopsticks and spoons, tissues, toothpicks, bottled water, jug of water, condiment tray (sliced green peppers, extra spicy chili powder), fish sauce, white pepper

RESTROOM
Squat toilet, no paper

Guaythiew Pik Gai Sai Nampheung

ก๋วยเตี๋ยวปีกไก่สายน้ำผึ้ง, 392/20 ถนนสุขุมวิท อยู่ในซอยฝั่งขวา ระหว่างซอย 20 และซอย 18

SHOPHOUSE, 392/20 SUKHUMVIT, SUKHUMVIT

This unassuming spot plastered with pictures of the Thai royal family serves up steaming bowls of a fairly unusual specialty: thick, short, hand-rolled noodles (*giem ee*) with chicken wings. The chicken boasts plenty of flavor and the broth is clear and refreshing.

GETTING THERE

392/20 Sukhumvit, on the right-hand side in the alleyway between Sukhumvit Sois 20 and 18
Tel 02-258-1958
Open 9.00–15.30 daily

SPECIALTY

Chinese-influenced *giem ee* (thick, short, hand-rolled noodles) in clear chicken broth with chicken wings, 35 baht (regular), 40 baht (special, bigger portion)
ก๋วยเตี๋ยวน้ำปีกไก่
เส้นเกี้ยมอี๋

OPTIONS

- Pork innards (intestine and liver), fish balls, pork balls
- Hand-rolled Chinese noodles (*giem ee*), thin noodles (*sen lek*), wide noodles (*sen yai*), egg noodles (*bamee*), glass vermicelli (*wunsen*)
- With broth (*nam*), without broth (*hang*), without noodles (*gow low*), broth separate (*nam yaek*), plain rice (*khao plow*), red fermented tofu noodles (*yen ta fo*)

SIDES

Fried wontons, fried fish skins, 20 baht/order

STANDARD TOPPINGS

Scallions, coriander and string beans instead of bean sprouts (otherwise known as Sukhothai-style

BEVERAGES

Iced coffee (*gafae yen*), coconut juice (*nam maphrao*), pickled plum juice (*nam buai*), tamarind juice (*nam makham*), roselle juice (*nam krajiep*), bael fruit juice (*nam matum*), 15 baht

SEATING Yes

ON THE TABLE

Tissues, toothpicks, bottled water, tea water, standard condiments (peanuts, dried chili powder, sugar, white vinegar with peppers), fish sauce, soy sauce

RESTROOM

Two rooms, squat toilets, no paper

Best for NOODLE SOUP

Saew

แซวก๋วยเตี๋ยวหมู (สุขุมวิท 49), ปากซอยสุขุมวิท 49 ตรงข้ามร้านโนริโกะ

SHOPHOUSE, SUKHUMVIT SOI 49, ACROSS FROM NORIKO, SUKHUMVIT

Arrive early at this popular lunchtime spot equipped with only a handful of seats and stay for a good bowl of noodles with a dash of taciturn, frequently disgruntled, service. It's also one of the few spots to offer tofu noodles.

GETTING THERE

At the entrance to Sukhumvit Soi 49, across from Noriko
Tel 02-258-7960
Open 7.00–16.30 daily

SPECIALTY

Egg noodles in tart-spicy (*tom yum*) broth served with pork, 30 baht, 40 baht (for special, bigger serving)
บะหมี่น้ำต้มยำหมูสูตร มะนาว

OPTIONS

- Pork (*moo*), fish balls (*luk chin pla*), tofu noodles (*guaythiew taohu*), red fermented tofu noodles (*yen ta fo*)
- Rice vermicelli (*sen mee*), thin noodles (*sen lek*), wide noodles (*sen yai*), egg noodles, wide or normal (*bamee, ban* or *glom*), glass vermicelli (*wunsen*), hand-rolled Chinese noodles (*giem ee*), without noodles (*gow low*)
- With broth (*nam*), without broth (*hang*), without noodles (*gow low*), broth separate (*nam yaek*), tart-spicy broth (*tom yum*), tart-spicy seasonings (*yum*)

NOTABLE EXTRAS

Deep-fried fish skins, 20 baht; tissues, 3 baht a pack

STANDARD TOPPINGS

Sugar, dried chilies, ground peanuts

BEVERAGES

Chinese-style black iced coffee (*olieng*), chrysanthemum tea (*geck huay*),- green tea with milk (*cha kiew sai nom*), longan juice (*nam lamyai*), sugarcane juice (*nam tansot*), tamarind juice (*nam makham*), soft drink/carbonated beverage (*nam atlom*), Vitamilk, 12 baht; pandanus leaf jelly (*woon baitoey*), 12 baht a glass, 65 baht a bottle

SEATING Yes

ON THE TABLE

Chopsticks, spoons, toothpicks, scissors, pencil, roll of paper to write orders, bottled water, jug of fresh water, condiment tray (pounded chili peppers, peanuts, sugar), fish sauce, vinegar with peppers, lime juice, fish skins

RESTROOM

Squat toilet, no paper

Best for PORK NOODLE SOUP

Bamee Soi 38

บะหมี่ปู-หมูแดง (สุขุมวิท 38), สุดซอยแยกทางขวา ในสุขุมวิทซอย 38

MOBILE VENDOR, SUKHUMVIT 38, SUKHUMVIT

Mild buttery egg noodles play the main role here, but deliciously flavored tender pork dumplings, barbecued pork and plump crab threaten to steal the show. Seating is right next to the food cart, so be prepared for a sweaty night.

GETTING THERE

Located towards the back of Soi 38 before the burger truck
Tel 089-679-9928
Open 20.30–3.00 daily

SPECIALTY

Chinese egg noodles (*bamee*), with pork dumplings and roasted red pork or crab (or both), 40–50 baht (regular), 50–60 baht (special, bigger serving)
บะหมี่ปูหมูแดง กับเกี๊ยวหมู

OPTIONS

- Roasted red pork (*moo dang*), crab (*pu*), or both (*ruam*)
- With or without dumplings (*giew*), dumplings only, broth only (*gow low*)
- With broth (*nam*), without broth (*hang*), without noodles (*gow low*), broth separate (*nam yaek*)

STANDARD TOPPINGS

Pickled cabbage, chopped coriander

BEVERAGES No

SEATING Yes

ON THE TABLE

Nothing (condiment tray served along with noodles)

RESTROOM No

Best for **EGG NOODLES**

83

Bamee Gua

บะหมี่กัว หลังสวน, 82 ถนนหลังสวน ฝั่งขวาของถนนใกล้สวนลุมพินี

SHOPHOUSE, 82 LANG SUAN ROAD, CLOSE TO LUMPINI PARK

It's hard to fault this well-known noodle stand, whether it's the hygiene (sparkling floors and tabletops), immaculately kept condiments or the food—well-loved, old-style Thai dishes hard to find elsewhere. The star of the show, however, is the homemade egg noodles.

GETTING THERE

On the right-hand side of Langsuan Road, close to where it meets Sarasin Road
Tel 02-251-6020, 02-251-9448
Open 9.00–15.00 daily except Sunday

Best for **EGG NOODLE SOUP**

SPECIALTY
Egg noodles with pork, chicken, squid, fish meatballs and dumplings, pickled turnip and lettuce (*bamee asawin*), 50 baht; noodles (*guaythiew*) in broth with accompaniments), 40–50 baht
บะหมี่อัศวิน

OPTIONS
- Noodles: egg noodles (*bamee*), rice vermicelli (*sen mee*), wide noodles (*sen yai*)
- Fish meatballs (*look chin pla*), fish dumplings (*giew pla*), barbecued pork (*moo yang*), chicken (*gai*), squid (*pla muk*)
- With broth (*nam*), without broth (*hang*), red fermented tofu noodles (*yen ta fo*)

NOTABLE EXTRAS
Flat rice noodles stir-fried with minced pork (*guaythiew moo sab*), with or without raw egg yolk (*kai dib*), 40 baht

BEVERAGES
Hot/cold coffee (*gafae ron/yen*), sweet iced green tea (*cha kiew*), iced milk tea (*cha yen*), iced cocoa (*coco yen*), 40 baht; black iced tea (*cha dum yen*), iced lemon tea (*cha manao*), iced milk (*nom yen*), iced honey/lime juice (*nampung pasom manao yen*), 35 baht; Italian soft drink with a range of fruit flavors: blue lemon, blueberry, strawberry, kiwi, apple or honey, 35 baht (5 baht for the addition of whipped cream to any drink)

SEATING Yes

ON THE TABLE
Tissues, condiment tray, Maggi sauce, fish sauce, Sriracha sauce

RESTROOM
Western toilet, with paper

Anamai

ลูกชิ้นอนามัย, 3 ซอยศูนย์วิจัย 7 ถนนเพชรบุรีตัดใหม่ หลังโรงพยาบาลหัวใจกรุงเทพ

SHOPHOUSE, 3 SOONVIJAI SOI 7, NEW PETCHBURI ROAD

Despite being part of a chain, Anamai is a must for diners who prize crystal-clear beef broth, solicitous service, and unquestionably hygienic surroundings. The roasted meatballs slathered in a sweet red chili sauce are also recommended.

GETTING THERE

Situated in the Bangkok Hospital compound in a small alleyway to the left of the four-way intersection as you enter the compound (next to the Bangkok Heart Hospital)
Tel 02-318-1606
Open 9.30–18.00 daily

SPECIALTY

Beef noodles in clear broth, 35 baht (regular), 45 baht (special, bigger serving)
ก๋วยเตี๋ยวเนื้อน้ำใส

OPTIONS

- Stewed beef (*nuea pleuy*), braised beef (*nuea thun*), boiled beef (*nuea sot*), beef meatballs (*luk chin*), liver (*thub*)
- Rice vermicelli (*sen mee*), wide noodles (*sen yai*), without noodles (*gow low*)
- With broth (*nam*), without broth (*hang*), without noodles (*gow low*), broth separate (*nam yaek*)

SIDES

Beef meatballs, boiled or roasted, with or without sweet red chili sauce, with or without "ends" (chewier, meatier meatballs), 35 baht for 5 sticks, 70 baht for 10 sticks

STANDARD TOPPINGS

Fried garlic, green onion, bean sprouts

BEVERAGES

Chinese-style black iced coffee (*olieng*), black iced tea (*cha dum yen*), roselle juice (*nam krajiep*), green or red Fanta (*nam kiew* or *nam dang*), 10 baht; Singha beer, 70–85 baht

SEATING Yes

ON THE TABLE

White chopsticks and Chinese spoons, tissues, toothpicks, jug of fresh water, clean condiment tray, small dipping bowls for sauces

RESTROOM

Clean bathroom with squat toilet, no paper; or use the cleaner and more numerous restrooms at the Bangkok Hospital next door

Best for
NOODLE
SOUP

Elvis Suki

เอลวิส สุกี้ 200/37 ซอยยศเส ถนนพลับพลาไชย

SHOPHOUSE, 200/37 SOI YODSAE, BETWEEN CHINATOWN AND HUALAMPHONG

Lovers of seafood flock to this unassuming shophouse (with an air-conditioned dining room a few doors away that opens later in the evening) at the stroke of 5 in order to snag one of the 15 grilled sea bass cooked every night.

GETTING THERE

Located on Soi Yodsae, the entrance to which is across the road from the Hua Chiew Hospital on Plabplachai Road
Tel 081-899-5533, 02-223-4979
Open 17.00–23.00 daily

SPECIALTY
Thai-style *sukiyaki*, 50–60 baht (depending on the seafood included)
สุกี้

Best for SUKIYAKI

OPTIONS
- Seafood (*talay*), chicken (*gai*), pork (*moo*), beef (*nuea*)
- With broth (*nam*), without broth (*hang*)

NOTABLE EXTRAS
Lemongrass-coated fish grilled in a banana leaf, market price, around 250 baht; grilled scallops with pork, 150 baht

BEVERAGES
Hot/cold coffee (*gafae ron/yen*), hot/cold tea (*cha ron/yen*), hot/cold black tea (*cha dum ron/cha dum yen*), iced lemon tea (*cha manao*), hot/cold Milo (Milo *ron/yen*), hot/cold Ovaltine (Ovaltine *ron/yen*), hot/cold cocoa (*coco ron/yen*), cold milk (*nom yen*), pickled plum juice (*nam buai*), roselle juice (*nam krajiep*), cold lime juice (*nam manao*), red/green soda (*nam dang/nam kiew*), 20 baht; Singha beer, 80 baht; Heineken beer, 100 baht

SEATING Yes

ON THE TABLE
Tissues, toothpicks, fish sauce, chili sauce, sugar, chili powder, pickled chilies in vinegar

RESTROOM
Squat toilet, no paper

Grilled Scallops

inspired by Elvis Suki

These grilled scallops are simple to prepare but have a big impact on the palate. Don't blanch at the sugar; it's what makes this dish so delicious.

4 servings

You will need

1 slice (about 60 g) pork neck
4 large scallops
2 tbs butter
2 large cloves garlic, finely minced
salt and pepper (to taste)
sugar

To make

1 Dry brine the pork by coating in salt for 15 minutes. Before using, pat dry.

2 Clean the scallops. Place a 1-inch-long piece of pork alongside each scallop on the shell. Season both with salt and pepper.

3 Make the garlic butter by mixing the garlic with the softened butter.

4 Dot with dollops of garlic butter and sprinkle both the scallops and pork with ¼ tsp sugar.

5 Broil in the oven for about 5 minutes, keeping a close eye so that the scallops do not burn.

6 Take out and serve while hot.

Chia Duck Noodles

ร้านเชี๊ยะ ก๋วยเตี๋ยวเป็ด, 2856 ถนนพระรามสี่ ตรงข้ามปั๊มเอสโซ่และร้านแมคโดนัลด์

SHOPHOUSE, 2856 RAMA IV ROAD, KHLONG TOEI

Delicious duck noodles and a pungent, aromatic duck stew are
what bring hordes of diners to this spot in the middle of nowhere
on a nondescript stretch of Rama IV Road. Go as close to
opening time as possible as the shop fills up in about 15 minutes.

GETTING THERE

Across the street from a gas station
and the entrance to Sukhumvit
Sois 22–24
Tel 02-671-3279
Open 19.30–midnight daily

SPECIALTY

Noodles in broth with stewed
duck, 35 baht
ก๋วยเตี๋ยวเป็ด

OPTIONS

- Noodles: *bamee* (egg
  noodles), rice vermicelli
  (*sen mee*), wide noodles
  (*sen yai*)
- Fish meatballs (*look chin
  pla*), fish dumplings (*giew
  pla*), barbecued pork (*moo*)
- With broth (*nam*), without

broth (*hang*), red fermented tofu noodles (*yen ta fo*),
noodles (*yang*), chicken
(*gai*), squid (*pla muk*)

NOTABLE EXTRAS

Stewed duck with five-
spice powder and Chinese
medicinal broth (*ped pullo
thun ya jeen*), 70 baht; with
bowl of rice, 5 baht. On
Sunday only, 10.00–14.00:
dim sum, Chinese-style
greens stew (*jab chai*), duck
on rice (*khao na ped*)

STANDARD TOPPINGS

Bean sprouts, scallions,
deep-fried garlic

BEVERAGES

Chinese-style black iced

coffee (*olieng*), black iced
tea (*cha dum yen*), chrysanthemum tea (*geck huay*),
pandanus jelly juice (*nam
woon baitoey*), roselle juice
with Chinese dates (*nam
krajiep sai pusaa jeen*), 10 baht

SEATING Yes

ON THE TABLE

Chopsticks and Chinese
spoons, tissues, toothpicks,
condiment tray

RESTROOM

Squat toilet, no paper,
relatively clean

Best for
EGG NOODLE SOUP

Gai Tawn Prathunam

ข้าวมันไก่ตอน ประตูน้ำ, หัวมุมเพชรบุรีซอย 30

SHOPHOUSE, CORNER OF PETCHBURI SOI 30, PRATUNAM

Hefty slices of chicken breast adorn delightfully fatty rice grains at this old chicken rice stand near the heart of Bangkok's shopping district. The food isn't the only retro thing about this place; so are the pink-shirted waitresses' grumpy faces.

GETTING THERE

At the corner of Petchburi Soi 30 and Petchburi Road
Tel 02-252-6325
Open 5.30–14.00, 17.00–2.00 daily

SPECIALTY

Hainanese chicken rice, 40 baht
ข้าวมันไก่ ไหหลำ

OPTIONS

- Just chicken (*gai tawn*), 60–120 baht
- Extra innards (liver, kidneys or heart) (*krueang nai*), 60–120 baht
- Just rice (with chicken fat) (*khao mun*), 10 baht

BEVERAGES

Bottled water, soft drink/ carbonated beverage (*nam atlom*), 10 baht

SEATING Yes

ON THE TABLE

Forks and spoons, tissues

RESTROOM

Squat toilet, no paper

Best for CHICKEN RICE

Northern and Central Thailand

Chiang Mai · Chiang Rai · Lampang · Sukhothai

Because of its cooler climate, the north of Thailand specializes in meatier fare that usually focuses on that other white meat, the noble pig. Pork, combined with salty, spicy and slightly bitter flavors, forms the backbone of much of the region's street food. It is often served deep-fried as meaty tidbits with sticky rice and chili paste or in a tomato-rich stew slathered over fermented rice noodles.

The North is also the home of one of the country's more beloved street food dishes: *khao soi*, or curried noodles. While the dish's origins are murky, Chiang Mai is now the center for this internationally renowned dish. The noodles are often served at Thai-Muslim establishments and, as a result, meat and chicken versions are easier to find than those featuring pork.

Noodles in pork broth

Chicken or beef curry noodles with chicken or beef satay

Beef noodles

Chiang Mai

Chiang Mai is the culinary jewel in northern Thailand's food crown. Blessed with a picturesque setting, welcoming people and a vibrant dining scene, the former capital of the North is a natural magnet for tourists from all over the world. Here, they can also dip a toe into exploring the meaty, filling wonders that make up northern Thai cuisine, which is distinct from its counterparts to the south and east.

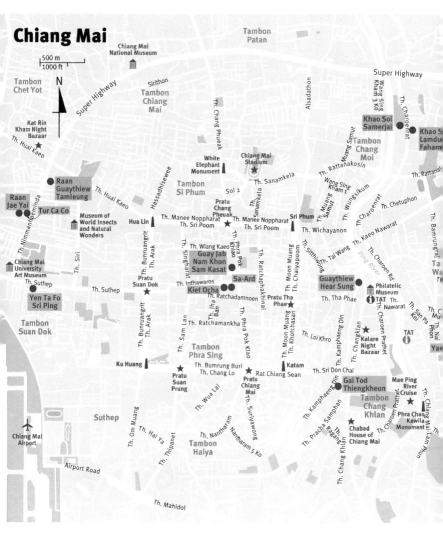

Khao Soi Samerjai

ข้าวซอยเสมอใจ, 391 ถนน เจริญราษฎร์

391 CHAROENRAT ROAD

Because the main attraction—the curried northern Thai noodles known as *khao soi*—is buried within a "food court" of northern Thai specials and other well-loved Thai dishes, Samerjai is a good one-stop shop for people with little time to sample all that Chiang Mai has to offer.

GETTING THERE

Located on Charoenrat Road, just down the street from Lamduan Faham
Tel 081-179-0999
Open 8.00–17.00 daily

Best for NOODLE SOUP

SPECIALTY

Northern Thai curried noodles (*khao soi*), 30 baht
ข้าวซอย

OPTIONS

With chicken (*gai*), beef (*nuea*), pork (*moo*), meatballs (*look chin*), pork ribs (*see krong moo*)

NOTABLE EXTRAS

Mon-style fermented rice noodles with tomato-minced pork stew (*khanom jeen nam ngeaw*), 30 baht

BEVERAGES

Chinese-style black iced coffee (*olieng*), black iced tea (*cha dum yen*), iced coffee/tea (*gafae/cha yen*), iced lemon tea (*cha manao*), chrysanthemum tea (*geck huay*), pennywort juice (*nam bai bua bok*), orange juice (*nam som*), guava juice (*nam farang*), sugarcane juice (*nam tansot*), roselle juice (*nam krajiep*), coconut juice (*nam maphrao*), mafueng juice (*nam mafueng*), longan juice (*nam lamyai*), fresh water (*nam plao*), 10 baht

SEATING Yes

ON THE TABLE

Tissues, condiment tray, fish sauce, sweet soy sauce, roasted chili paste

RESTROOM

Western toilet, no flush, with paper

93

Yen Ta Fo Sri Ping

เย็นตาโฟศรีพิงค์, 231 ถนนสุเทพ บนถนนใหญ่

231 SUTHEP ROAD

Here you'll find deliciously saucy noodles topped with seafood, chili and the tart, mouth-puckering flavor that lovers of *yen ta fo* (red fermented tofu noodles) yearn for. Service is less than welcoming but you can console yourself with the relative cleanliness of your surroundings.

GETTING THERE

On the main road, not far from the Chiang Mai University Art Museum
Open 9.00–17.00 daily

Best for **NOODLE SOUP**

SPECIALTY

Red fermented tofu noodles (*yen ta fo*), 35 baht, 40 baht (special serving)
ก๋วยเตี๋ยวเย็นตาโฟ

OPTIONS

- Red fermented tofu noodles (*yen ta fo*), fish meatballs (*luk chin pla*), mixed pork (*moo sab*)
- Wide noodles (*sen yai*), thin noodles (*sen lek*), glass vermicelli (*wunsen*), egg noodles (*bamee*)
- With broth (*nam*), without broth (*hang*), without noodles (*gow low*), with tart-spicy broth (*tom yum*)

BEVERAGES

Chinese-style black iced coffee (*olieng*), iced lemon tea (*cha manao*), 15 baht; iced tea/coffee (*cha/gafae yen*), 20 baht; sugarcane juice (*nam tansot*), guava juice (*nam farang*), pennywort juice, (*nam bai bua bok*), 15–40 baht; soft drink/carbonated beverage (*nam atlom*), 12 baht; fresh water (*nam plao*),10 baht

SEATING Yes

ON THE TABLE
Tissues, toothpicks, jug of fresh water, fish sauce, powdered peanuts, sugar, chili powder, pickled chilies

RESTROOM
Squat toilet, no flush, paper at entrance

Raan Guaythiew Tamleung

ร้านก๋วยเตี๋ยวตำลึง, 14 ถนนนิมมานเหมินทร์ ซอย 1 ฝั่งขวา

14 NIMMANHAEMINDA SOI 1

The only noodle shop on a road full of upscale design stores,
this one specializes in minced pork noodles with
blanched *tamleung* (a spinach-like green) leaves. A rice and curry
counter also offers everything from the ubiquitous northern Thai
curried noodles known as *khao soi* to green curry.

GETTING THERE

On the right-hand side of
Nimmanhaeminda Soi 1, about
50 meters along
Tel 053-224-741, 085-714-9161
Open 8.30–15.00 daily

SPECIALTY

Noodles with minced pork, 35–
40 baht (depending on size)
เกี๋ยวเตี๋ยวหมู

OPTIONS

● Noodles: wide noodles (*sen yai*), thin noodles (*sen lek*), rice vermicelli (*sen mee*), egg noodles (*bamee*), wontons (*giew*), glass vermicelli (*wunsen*), without noodles (*gow low*)
● Protein: minced pork (*moo sup*), blanched pork (*moo sod*), innards (*krueang nai*), mixed pork (*ruammit*)
● Broth: regular (*tamada*), spicy lemongrass (*tom yum*), no broth (*hang*), no broth with *tom yum* seasoning (*hang yum*)

NOTABLE EXTRAS

Rice with curry, 20 baht; with
two kinds of curry, 25–30 baht

BEVERAGES

Chinese-style black iced
coffee (*olieng*), old-fashioned
coffee (*gafae sod*), chrysanthemum tea (*geck huay*),
black iced tea (*cha dum yen*),
iced milk tea (*cha yen*),
sugarcane juice (*nam tansot*),
pennywort juice (*nam bai bua bok*), guava juice (*nam farang*), pickled plum juice
(*nam buai*), lemongrass
juice (*nam takrai*), orange
juice (*nam som*), roselle juice
(*nam krajiep*), tamarind
juice (*nam makham*), lychee
juice (*nam linchi*), all 15 baht

SEATING Yes

ON THE TABLE

Chopsticks and spoons,
tissues, toothpicks, bottled
water, condiment tray, fish
sauce, fish sauce with
chopped chilies

RESTROOM

Western toilet, no flush, no
paper

Best for
PORK
NOODLE
SOUP

Guay Jab Nam Khon Sam Kasat

ก๋วยจั๊บน้ำข้นสามกษัตริย์, ตรงข้ามอนุสาวรีย์สามกษัตริย์

PHRA POK KHIAO ROAD

While the namesake dish earns kudos for its herbal-inflected charms,
the star of the stall might well be the *khao moo grob* (rice with crispy pork),
a bed of white rice crowned with a crackling plateful of deep-fried pig.

GETTING THERE

Across the street from the Three Kings Monument in Phra Pok Khiao Road
Tel 086-923-6378
Open 7.30–15.00 daily except public holidays

SPECIALTY

Chinese hand-rolled noodles in pork broth (*guay jab*), 50 baht; crispy pork rice (*khao moo grob*), 50 baht
ก๋วยจั๊บ และข้าวหมูกรอบ

NOTABLE EXTRAS

Pork and beef broth (*gow low*), 50 baht; crispy pork (*moo grob*), 50–70 baht; pork intestines (*sai moo*), 50–70 baht; sausage of minced pork (*luk lok*), 50 baht; plain rice, 5 baht

BEVERAGES

Chinese-style black iced coffee (*olieng*), iced fresh coffee (*gafae sod yen*), chrysanthemum tea (*geck huay*), black iced tea (*cha dum yen*), iced milk tea (*cha yen*), sugarcane juice (*nam tansot*), pennywort juice (*nam bai bua bok*), guava juice (*nam farang*), coconut juice (*nam maphrao*), pickled plum juice (*nam buai*), lemongrass juice (*nam takrai*), orange juice (*nam som*), palm sugar juice, all 20 baht

Best for
PORK NOODLE SOUP

SEATING Yes

ON THE TABLE

Tissues, toothpicks, fresh water, tea water, fish sauce, light soy sauce, sugar, pepper, chili powder, pickled chilies

RESTROOM
Squat toilet, no flush, no paper

98

Guaythiew Hear Sung

ก๋วยเตี๋ยวเฮียสั่ง, ในซอยหลังวัดแขก

IN THE SOI BEHIND THE INDIAN TEMPLE (WAT KAEK)

This packed shophouse stall specializes in fish meatball noodles, a category that frequently confuses pescatarians because slivers of pork flesh and innards are often included. The specialty dish here is no exception but the meaty bits are what make the dish.

GETTING THERE

Located in the alleyway behind the Indian Temple (Wat Kaek)
Tel 053-233-613, 081-952-0744
Open 7.30–16.00 daily

Best for
FISH NOODLE SOUP

SPECIALTY
Fish meatball noodles, 25 baht, 30 baht (special serving)
ก๋วยเตี๋ยวปลา

OPTIONS
- Wide noodles (*sen yai*), thin noodles (*sen lek*), egg noodles (*bamee*), rice vermicelli (*sen mee*), glass vermicelli (*wunsen*), 25–30 baht
- Pork dumplings (*giew*), hand-rolled Chinese noodles (*giem ee*), 30–35 baht
- With broth (*nam*), without broth (*hang*), without noodles (*gow low*), 30–35 baht
- Red fermented tofu noodles (*yen ta fo*), 25–30 baht
- Curried noodles (*khao soi*), 30–35 baht

BEVERAGES
Iced coffee (*gafae yen*), iced tea (*cha yen*), lime tea, black iced tea (*cha dum yen*), chrysanthemum tea (*geck huay*), pickled plum juice (*nam buai*), pennywort juice (*nam bai bua bok*), guava juice (*nam farang*), lemongrass juice (*nam takrai*), orange juice (*nam som*), soft drink/carbonated beverage (*nam atlom*), all 12 baht; ice, 1 baht

SEATING Yes

ON THE TABLE
Tissues, toothpicks, jug of pandanus leaf-flavored water, fish sauce, powdered peanuts, sugar, chili powder, pickled chilies, mashed chilies for *khao soi*

RESTROOM
Squat toilet, no flush, no paper

Kiet Ocha

เกียรติโอชา, 41–43 ถนนอินทวโรรส

41–43 INTAWOROS ROAD

Feel like a simple plate of *khao mun gai*, or Hainanese-style chicken rice?
This shop, owned by a Thai lottery winner who still patrols the
shop as before, specializes in both the boiled and fried versions
as well as crispy pork on rice.

GETTING THERE

On Intaworos Road, next to Sa-Ard
fish noodle stand
Tel 053-327-292-3
Open 8.00–14.00 daily

SPECIALTY

Boiled or fried chicken rice,
30 baht
ข้าวมันไก่

OPTIONS

- Single portion, 30 baht;
  plate of sliced chicken or
  pork for sharing, 40, 50, 70,
  90, 120 baht (depending
  on size)
- With innards—gizzards,
  liver, blood (*gub krueang
  nai*) or without (*mai ow
  krueang nai*)

NOTABLE EXTRAS

Pork or chicken satay, 40, 50,
70, 90, 120 baht (depending on
number of sticks); rice, 5 baht

BEVERAGES

Fresh water (*nam plao*), 5
baht/bottle; U-Thai-Tip water,
tea water (*nam cha*), free

SEATING Yes

ON THE TABLE

U-Thai-Tip water, tea water,
bottled water, tissues,
toothpicks

RESTROOM

Western toilet, no flush, with
paper

Best for CHICKEN RICE

Sa-Ard

สะอาด, 33–35 ถนนอินทวโรรส

33–35 INTAWOROS ROAD

The packed shophouse next to the famed Kiet Ocha bears a reputation for some of the tastiest fish meatballs in the city, a reputation that is well-deserved. The most popular dish by far remains the mixed fish meatballs in fish broth.

GETTING THERE

On Intaworos Road, next to Kiet Ocha chicken rice stand
Tel 053-327-261, 053-233-613, 089-140-2227
Open 7.00–18.00 daily

Best for FISH NOODLE SOUP

SPECIALTY

Fish meatball noodles, 40 baht, 50 baht (special serving)

ก๋วยเตี๋ยวปลา

OPTIONS

- Wide noodles (*sen yai*), thin noodles (*sen lek*), egg noodles (*bamee*), rice vermicelli (*sen mee*), glass vermicelli (*wunsen*), 40–50 baht
- Fish dumplings (*giew pla*), 40–50 baht with broth (*nam*), without broth (*hang*), without noodles (*gow low*), 50–60 baht
- Red fermented tofu noodles (*yen ta fo*), 40–50 baht
- Spicy lemongrass (*tom yum*), 40–50 baht

NOTABLE EXTRAS

Poached fish (*nuea pla sod luak jim*), 60 baht; mixed meatballs with dipping sauce (*luk chin luak ruam nam jim*), 60 baht; deep-fried fish skins (*nung pla*), 20 baht/bag

BEVERAGES

Iced coffee/tea (*gafae/cha yen*), 25 baht; iced lemon tea (*cha manao*), roselle juice (*nam krajiep*), guava juice (*nam farang*), tamarind juice (*nam makham*), lime juice (*nam manao*), soft drink/carbonated beverage (*nam atlom*), 12 baht; fresh water (*nam plao*), 5 baht/bottle

SEATING Yes

ON THE TABLE

Tissues, toothpicks, bottled water, deep-fried fish skins, fish sauce, two types of pickled peppers in vinegar, sugar, chili powder, sweets menu

RESTROOM

Squat toilet, no flush, no paper

Khao Soi Lamduan Faham

ข้าวซอยลำดวนฟ้าห้าม, 352/22 ถนนเจริญรัตน์

352/22 CHAROENRAT ROAD

Arguably the most famous *khao soi* (curried noodle) shop in Chiang Mai, Lamduan, named after the original owner, claims to have been the first to come up with the northern Thai curried noodle dish. It's unclear whether this is true or not but the broth here argues a convincing case.

GETTING THERE

Located on Charoenrat Road, near Khao Soi Samerjai. Both are famous vendors so ask any local for directions if you get lost
Tel 053-243-519, 083-156-1916
Open 8.00–17.00 daily

SPECIALTY

Northern Thai curried noodles (*khao soi*), 30–40 baht (depending on size)

OPTIONS

With pork (*moo*), beef (*nuea*), chicken (*gai*), spareribs (see *krong moo*), fish (*pla*)

NOTABLE EXTRAS

Mon-style fermented rice noodles with tomato-minced pork stew (*khanom jeen nam ngeaw*), 30–40 baht (depending on size)

BEVERAGES

Iced tea/coffee (*cha/gafae yen*), 15 baht; iced lemon tea (*cha manao*), black iced tea (*cha dum yen*), chrysanthemum tea (*geck huay*), 10 baht; butterfly pea juice (*nam dok anchan*), 15 baht; longan juice (*nam lamyai*), roselle juice (*nam krajiep*), guava juice (*nam farang*), pennywort juice (*nam bai bua bok*), 10 baht; carrot juice (*nam carrot*), 20 baht; watermelon shake (*thangmo bun*), 30 baht

SEATING Yes

ON THE TABLE

Chopsticks, spoons, tissues, bottled water, fish sauce, sweet soy sauce, brown sugar, chili paste, vinegar

RESTROOM

Western toilet, no flush, no paper

Best for NOODLE SOUP

Khao Soi Gai

inspired by Khao Soi Lamduan Faham

There are few street food dishes as popular as *khao soi*, a northern Thai curried noodle dish, and few street vendors as popular as Lamduan Faham in Chiang Mai. To ensure that the curried "sauce" has the right consistency (think soup, not curry), don't hesitate to add more hot water to achieve the desired consistency.

4 servings

You will need

500 g chicken breast, cubed
½ cup ginger, peeled and cubed
1 cup shallots, cubed
4 bundles egg noodles, fresh
250 ml vegetable oil
1 tbs dark soy sauce
½ tsp chili powder
50 g yellow curry paste
500 ml coconut milk
3 tbs sugar
3 tbs soy sauce
1 tsp salt
3 scallions and 1 bunch coriander, sliced (for garnish)
pickled cabbage, chopped (for garnish)
2–3 shallots, sliced (for garnish)
1 lime, cut into wedges (for garnish)
sugar, fish sauce and chili powder (for seasoning)

To make

1 Mix the ginger and shallots in a blender or food processor, dampening with a few tbs water until a thick paste is formed.

2 To make the deep-fried noodle garnish, take one bundle of fresh egg noodles and shake out excess flour. Fry in 200 ml hot vegetable oil until they are a deep golden color. Drain on paper towels.

3 Blanch the remaining noodles by placing each bundle in a strainer and immersing in boiling water. Shake for a minute or so with chopsticks, then plunge each bundle in ice water to stop the cooking process. Drain and season with 1 tbs dark soy sauce and 1 tbs vegetable oil.

4 To make the chili oil used to season the dish, "sprout" the chili powder in ¼ cup oil, then set aside.

5 To make the curried "sauce", fry the ginger and shallot mixture with 1 tbs water for a minute, then add the yellow curry paste. Stir-fry until fragrant. Add the chicken cubes and cook until seared. Then add the coconut milk, ensuring that it has a "soupy" consistency. Thin with water, if necessary. Taste and season with 3 tbs sugar, 3 tbs soy sauce and 1 tsp salt. Taste again and correct the seasoning. Add a splash of coconut cream at the end if you like.

6 Place the noodles in a bowl. Cover with the sauce and garnish with the deep-fried noodles, scallions, coriander, cabbage, shallots and wedge of lime. Season with sugar, fish sauce and chili powder as you see fit.

Yaowapa (Kluay Tod Bat Queue)

กล้วยทอดบัตรคิวเยาวภา, 20/6 ถนนกองทราย ตำบลวัดเกตุ อำเภอเมือง

20/6 KONGSAI ROAD, TAMBOL WAT KET, AMPHOR MUANG

This fried banana stand, named after the indefatigable Yaowapa who deep-fries her creations in two giant oil-filled woks, is so popular that you must pick up a number and stand in line before placing your order.

GETTING THERE

Located on Kongsai Road, near the Prince Royal College
Tel 053-240-799
Open 8.00–17.00 daily

SPECIALTY
Fried bananas (*gluay tod*), 15 baht for small, 20 baht for medium, 30 baht for large
กล้วยทอด

OPTIONS
- Fried bananas (*gluay tod*)
- A coconut-like vegetable, cut into chips and fried (*glawy tod*)
- Fried sweet potatoes (*mun ted tod*)
- Bananas in sweet batter with coconut flakes (*khao mao*)

BEVERAGES No

SEATING No

RESTROOM No

Tur Ca Co

ตือคาโค, ตรงข้ามประตูเชียงใหม่

ACROSS FROM CHIANG MAI GATE

The deep-fried rounds of taro and batter known in Chiang Mai as *tur ca co* are actually a Teochew snack, here adapted to Thai taste with crispier pieces and a thicker tamarind sauce. This blink and you'll miss it stall has come up with its own kind that is crunchier and thinner.

GETTING THERE

Located on the left-hand side of Nimmanhaeminda Road across from Chiang Mai Gate
Tel 085-869-0234
Open 8.00–20.30 daily

SPECIALTY
Deep-fried taro and batter rounds (*tur ca co*); deep-fried tofu (*taohu tod*), 15 baht for 6 pieces
อาหารแนะนำ: ตือคาโคและ
เต้าหู้ทอด

BEVERAGES No

SEATING No

RESTROOM No

Best for
SNACKS

Gai Tod Thiengkheun

(Midnight Fried Chicken) ไก่ทอดเที่ยงคืน, ถนนกำแพงดิน ด้านซ้าย

สังเกตจากคิวคนที่ยืนคอยนอกร้านจนถึงเที่ยงคืน

KAMPHAENG DIN ROAD

In this city it is still possible to stuff one's face after midnight with delicious northern Thai-style fried meat, thanks to this enterprising and perpetually packed stall. Midnight Fried Chicken also excels in frying up delicious three-layer pork belly (*moo sam chan*).

GETTING THERE

Located on the left-hand side of Kamphaeng Din Road, noticeable from the queue of people lined up outside at midnight
Tel 053-211-069
Open midnight–5.00 daily

Best for ISAAN DISHES

SPECIALTY

Fried chicken (*gai tod*), 50–55 baht (small plate), 100–110 baht (large plate); three-layer pork (*moo sam chan*), 45 baht (small plate), 90 baht (large plate)
ไก่ทอดและหมูสามชั้นทอด

NOTABLE EXTRAS

Boiled duck egg (*kai thom*), 7 baht; sticky rice (*khao niew*), 10–20 baht

BEVERAGES

Self-service fresh water in a jug at the back

SEATING

Yes

ON THE TABLE

Order slips, pen, tissues, fish sauce

RESTROOM

Squat toilet, no flush, no paper

Raan Jae Yai

ร้านเจ๊ใหญ่, 28/4 ถนนนิมมานเหมินทร์ ซอย 8 ฝั่งซ้าย

28/4 NIMMANHAEMINDA ROAD, SOI 8

Great vegetarian renditions of tried and true Thai favorites are on offer at this made-to-order stand as well as more "traditional" versions in case you're saddled with some die-hard omnivores. A wide range of dishes means you will never leave on an empty stomach.

GETTING THERE

Located on the left-hand side of Nimmanhaeminda Soi 8, after the Myanmar food stall
Tel 053-220-373
Open 9.30–20.00 daily

SPECIALTY

Vegetarian stir-fried flat rice noodles (*guaythiew kua gai*), 30 baht; vegetarian red curry with tofu and vegetables (*gaeng ped*) with rice, 50 baht; vegetarian sweet yellow curry with tofu and vegetables (*gaeng gari*) with rice, 50 baht
ก๋วยเตี๋ยวคั่วไก่เจ (30 บาท) ข้าวแกงเผ็ดเต้าหู้กับผัก (50 บาท) และข้าวแกงกะหรี่เต้าหู้กับผัก (50 บาท)

BEVERAGES

Passionfruit juice (*nam saowarot*), 35 baht; soft drink/carbonated beverage (*nam atlom*), 10 baht

SEATING Yes

ON THE TABLE

Tissues, toothpicks, jugs of fresh water, condiment tray, Maggi sauce

RESTROOM No

Best for **VEGETARIAN DISHES**

Chiang Rai

Thailand's northernmost major city, Chiang Rai, draws visitors seeking bucolic scenery coupled with a hearty dose of northern Thai culture. Alas, that culture still cleaves to a traditional Thai timetable: while restaurants and vendors bustle in the daytime, Chiang Rai's nights are considerably quieter than those spent in its younger sister to the south, Chiang Mai. Nonetheless, curried rice noodles, pork-heavy stews and beef noodles are all stand-out dishes here.

Nuea Wua Rot Yiem

เนื้อวัวรสเยี่ยม, 421/4–5 ถนนบรรพปราการ

421/4–5 BANPHAPRAKAN ROAD

Despite being resolutely pro-Thaksin (Chiang Rai locals call the place *Guaythiew nuea suea dang*, or "red shirt beef noodles"), this shophouse attracts diners from both sides of the political divide on the back of its flavorful beef bits and clear beef broth.

Best for BEEF NOODLE SOUP

GETTING THERE

Located on the main road running through town, Banphaprakan Road, near the clock tower
Tel 053-601-190
Open 8.00–15.00 daily

SPECIALTY

Beef noodles, 50–80 baht (depending on size and topping)
ก๋วยเตี๋ยวเนื้อ

OPTIONS

- Noodles: rice vermicelli (*sen mee*), thin noodles (*sen lek*), wide noodles (*sen yai*), without noodles (*gow low*)
- Protein: stewed beef (*nuea thun*), meatballs (*look chin*), blanched beef (*nuea sod*), innards (*krueang nai*), everything (*ruam*)
- Broth: with broth (*nam*), without broth (*hang*)

SEATING Yes

ON THE TABLE

Chopsticks and spoons, small bowls, toothpicks, tissues, bottled water, fish sauce, dried chili, sugar, pickled chilies in vinegar

BEVERAGES

Black iced tea (*cha dum yen*), chrysanthemum tea (*geck huay*), roselle juice (*nam krajiep*), pickled plum juice (*nam buai*), herbal drink similar to lemongrass juice (*grachai dum*), 15 baht; fresh water (*nam plao*), 6 baht for small bottle, 14 baht for large

RESTROOM

Western toilet, no flush, no paper

Khao Soi Islam

ข้าวซอยอิสลาม, ถนนงำเมือง

NAM (NGAM) MUANG ROAD

This shophouse featuring "Chinese noodles" proudly proclaims its long history (open since 1929) and the deliciousness of its curried noodles. While the noodles are good enough—made with the coconut milk added in stages like a curry—the real star here is the chicken biryani.

GETTING THERE

Located on the left-hand side of Nam Muang Road
Tel 053-712-165, 084-041-7836
Open 8.00–15.00 daily

SPECIALTY
Curried noodles (*khao soi*),
30 baht; chicken biryani
(*khao mok gai*), 35 baht
ข้าวซอย

OPTIONS
For curried noodles (*khao soi*):
beef (*nuea*) or chicken (*gai*)

SEATING Yes

Best for NOODLE SOUP

ON THE TABLE
Chopsticks and spoons, tissues,
toothpicks, bottled water, sweet soy
sauce, chili paste, sugar, fish sauce,
Thai-style Sriracha sauce, vinegar

BEVERAGES
Black iced tea (*cha dum yen*), guava
juice (*nam farang*), tamarind juice
(*nam makham*), 10 baht

RESTROOM
Avoid

Khanom Jeen Nam Ngeaw Pa Suk

ขนมจีนน้ำเงี้ยวป้าสุข, ถนนสันโค้งน้อย รอบเวียง

5 SANKHONGNOI ROAD, TAMBOL, ROBWIANG

This long-standing stall serves a specialty influenced by the Shan, an ethnic minority in Burma. Known as *khanom jeen nam ngeaw*, the dish comprises fermented Mon-style rice noodles slathered in a rich sauce of either beef or pork, studded with chilies, cherry tomatoes and dried *ngeaw* blossoms.

GETTING THERE
Located midway along Sankhongnoi Road
Tel 053-752-471
Open 8.00–15.00 daily

SPECIALTY
Mon-style fermented rice noodles with tomato-minced pork stew (*khanom jeen nam ngeaw*), 30–35 baht
ขนมจีนน้ำเงี้ยว

OPTIONS
- Protein: pork (*moo*), beef (*nuea*)
- Noodles: fermented rice noodles (*khanom jeen*), thin noodles (*sen lek*), wide noodles (*sen yai*)
- Broth (if with rice noodles): with broth (*nam*), without broth (*hang*)

NOTABLE EXTRAS
Khao ganjin, 10 baht

SEATING Yes

ON THE TABLE
Tissues, soft drink/carbonated beverage, lime juice, fish sauce, white vinegar, chili paste, pickled peppers, sugar, pork rinds

BEVERAGES
Black iced tea (*cha dum yen*), iced milk tea (*cha yen*), Coke, 10 baht

RESTROOM
Western toilet, with paper

Best for FERMENTED RICE NOODLE

Khanom Jeen Nam Ngeaw

inspired by
Khanom Jeen Nam Ngeaw Pa Suk

This recipe is a cherished family favorite, referred to as "Thai spaghetti" by my father, who made it for us periodically during our time in the US. The version at Khanom Jeen Nam Ngeaw Pa Suk in Chiang Rai, my father's hometown, comes closest to the taste of the dish he made at home. However, a few ingredients are difficult to obtain. If you are able to source them or order them from Thailand, please do so as there are no good substitutes for these ingredients.

10–12 servings

You will need

1 kg pork bones
1 kg minced pork
300 g *nam ngeaw* chili paste (a mix of chilies, garlic and shallots)
2 pieces pork blood, cubed
2 kg tomatoes, cubed or sliced if cherry tomatoes
100 g *dok ngeaw*, a broomstick-like herb, soaked briefly in hot water
2 discs *tua now* (fermented brown beans, a common ingredient in northern Thai cuisine) or
2 tbs Chinese brown bean sauce
2 tsp salt
4 pork bouillon cubes
¼ cup soy sauce
vegetable oil (for frying)
10 bundles *khanom jeen*, a Mon-style fermented rice noodle
pickled mustard greens, chopped (for garnish)
5 limes, cut into wedges (for garnish)
5 scallions and 4 bunches coriander, sliced (for garnish)
100 g bean sprouts, washed (for garnish)

To make

1 In 2 inches of boiling water, stew the pork bones for 2 hours.
2 Fry the chili paste in 1 tbs oil until fragrant.
3 Add the minced pork and fry until cooked.
4 Add the mince to the pork bones. Clean out the mince pot by adding 1 inch of water and then adding to the pork bones.
5 Add the pork blood and tomatoes.
6 Add the *ngeaw* blossoms. Skim the foam from the surface from time to time.
7 Grill the fermented bean discs by placing in a hot dry frying pan, one at a time, until fragrant and the color darkens (if using Chinese brown bean sauce, skip this and the following steps).
8 Pound the discs ito a powder in a mortar and pestle. Add to the pot.
9 Season with salt, pork bouillon cubes, soy sauce and Chinese brown bean sauce, if using.
10 Add more water until the level is a couple of inches from the top of the pot. Bring to the boil, then lower to a simmer for 2 hours, uncovered.
11 Taste and adjust the seasoning.
12 Place the *khanom jeen* (fermented rice noodles) in a bowl and cover with the sauce. Garnish with pickled greens, lime, scallions, coriander and bean sprouts. Serve immediately.

Lampang

Quiet, unassuming Lampang might not be a natural place for a culinary stop, but this small northern Thai city does enjoy an undercover reputation as a major destination for Thai lovers of the local cuisine at all hours of the day and night. Its markets bristle with quality northern Thai-style sausages and chili pastes, while customers throng the noodle vendors.

Niyom Pochana

นิยมโภชนา, หน้าวัดเมืองสาสน์ ถนนเจริญเมือง

CHAROENMUANG ROAD

This noodle stand is hard to find, but worth it. If you like clear beef broth with soft noodles and hefty, flavorful meatballs, this is the place for you. Known all over town for its delicious noodles, this stall draws in locals all day long.

GETTING THERE
Located right in front of Muangsat Temple on Charoenmuang Road
Tel 089-261-4282
Open 10.30–16.30 daily

Best for **BEEF NOODLE SOUP**

SPECIALTY
Beef noodles, 30–35 baht (depending on size)
ก๋วยเตี๋ยวลูกชิ้นเนื้อ

OPTIONS
- Noodles: wide noodles (*sen yai*), rice vermicelli (*sen mee*), without noodles (*gow low*)
- Protein: beef meatballs (*look chin wua*), pork meatballs (*look chin moo*), boiled pork (*moo thom*), blanched beef (*nuea sod*), stewed beef (*nuea thoon*)
- Broth: with broth (*nam*), without broth (*hang*)

SEATING Yes

ON THE TABLE
Tissues, toothpicks, tea water, condiment tray, fish sauce, roasted chili oil, pickled chilies in vinegar

BEVERAGES
Roselle juice (*nam krajiep*), longan juice (*nam lamyai*), sugarcane juice (*nam tansot*), lemongrass juice (*nam takrai*), tamarind juice (*nam makham*), 12 baht

RESTROOM
Squat, no flush, no paper; look for a better alternative

117

Khao Soi Islam

ข้าวซอยอิสลาม, ถนนปงสนุก

PRASANUK (PONGSANUK) ROAD

Unlike at other *khao soi* stalls, the curried noddles here come in only two varieties—beef and chicken—and the coconut milk is cooked into the broth, not added at the end. The result is a more curry-like broth, with an unctuous consistency and more subtle flavor.

GETTING THERE

Located on Prasanuk Road, close to the Watermelon Rice Cracker factory
Tel 054-227-826
Open 9.00–14.30 daily

SPECIALTY

Northern Thai curried noodles (*khao soi*), 30–40 baht (depending on size)
ข้าวซอย

OPTIONS

Beef (*nuea*), chicken (*gai*)

NOTABLE EXTRAS

Beef (*nuea*) or chicken (*gai*) satay, 30 baht

SEATING Yes

ON THE TABLE

Tissues, fish sauce, sweet soy sauce, sugar, roasted chili paste

BEVERAGES

Iced coffee (*gafae yen*), iced milk tea (*cha yen*), iced milk (*nom yen*), 15 baht

RESTROOM

Squat toilet, no flush, no paper

Best for
NOODLE SOUP

Choose chicken or beef.

Chicken and Beef Satay

inspired by Khao Soi Islam

This recipe is very easy but requires a fair bit of preparation. It has been adapted for the oven but can be cooked on a grill.

4 servings

For the satay
satay sticks
300 g beef tenderloin, sliced thinly
300 g chicken thigh, sliced
1 tbs curry powder
½ cup coconut milk
1 tbs honey
2 tbs fish sauce
2 tbs soy sauce
3 garlic cloves, smashed
2 shallots, smashed
1–3 red chilies, crushed

To make
1 Soak the satay sticks in water.
2 Combine all the ingredients except the meat to make the marinade. Pour half the marinade over the beef and the other half over the chicken and put in the refrigerator for at least an hour.
3 When ready to cook, turn the oven to high and thread the meat onto the sticks. Place the sticks on an oiled baking sheet (or, ideally, a cooling rack on a baking sheet) and place closest to the heat in the oven. Grill for 5–7 minutes, turning the sticks over halfway through until the meat is browned and slightly charred at the edges.

For Chris's peanut sauce
1½ cups dry roasted peanuts (unsalted) or ¾ cup smooth peanut butter
½ cup coconut milk
3 garlic cloves, minced
1 tsp soy sauce
1½ tsp sesame oil
1 tbs brown sugar (omit if using peanut butter)
1 tbs fish sauce (or to taste)
2 tsp tamarind paste (or lime juice)
1 tsp Sriracha sauce or Thai chili sauce
¼ cup water (if needed to thin the mixture)

To make
Process until smooth. Taste and adjust seasonings until there is a balance between tangy, spicy, sweet and salty.

For the cucumber-shallot relish
1 small cucumber, washed and sliced
3 red chilies, sliced
3 shallots, sliced
½ cup rice vinegar
1 tbs white sugar

To make
Combine all the ingredients making sure the sugar dissolves in the vinegar. Serve with the satay, peanut sauce and, if you wish, toasted white bread.

119

Sukhothai

Thailand's capital city before Ayutthaya and Bangkok, Sukhothai still showcases verdant central Thai greenery interspersed with shots of Thai high culture. Set in a particularly fertile part of the country, Sukhothai abounds in rice, vegetables and limes, all of which are put to good use in the local specialties. A must-try here is the city's famous soup noodles, cooked in a pork broth and topped with green beans and peanuts.

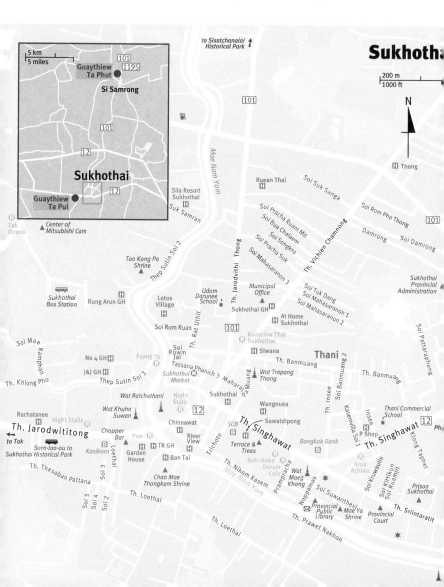

Guaythiew Ta Pui

ก๋วยเตี๋ยวตาปุย, ถนนจรดวิถีถ่อง, บ้านกล้วย

JARODWITITONG ROAD, BAAN GLUAY

Although the original owner has passed away, her family carries on the tradition of reliable (and relatively hygienic) Sukhothai-style egg crepe and, of course, the famous Sukhothai noodles.

GETTING THERE

Located directly on Jarowititong Road, Baan Gluay
Tel 055-620-435
Open 8.00–16.00 daily

SPECIALTY

Sukhothai noodles (*guay-thiew Sukhothai*) 25–30 baht, depending on options
ก๋วยเตี๋ยวสุโขทัย

OPTIONS

- For Sukhothai noodles: If not specified, vendor will use thin noodles (*sen lek*), also option of spicy lemon-grass broth (*tom yum*), with broth (*nam*), without broth (*hang*), minced pork (*moo sab*), red barbecued pork (*moo dang*) or both (*ruam*)
- For spicy lemongrass noodles (not Sukhothai): thin noodles (*sen lek*), rice vermicelli (*sen mee*), with broth (*nam*), without broth (*hang*), pork ribs (*si krong moo*), stewed chicken leg (*nong gai thun*), pig innards (*krueang nai moo*), marinated pork (*moo mak*), pig/fish meatballs (*look chin moo/ pla*), all pig parts (*ruammitr moo*)

NOTABLE EXTRAS

Pad Thai with marinated pork (*pad Thai moo mak*), 30–50

baht; Sukhothai-style egg crepe (*khanom bueang Sukhothai*), 30–50 baht

SEATING Yes

ON THE TABLE

Chopsticks and spoons, tissues, fresh water, condiment tray, sugar

BEVERAGES

Chinese-style black iced coffee (*olieng*), old-fashioned iced coffee (*gafae boran*), iced lemon tea (*cha manao*), iced chrysanthemum tea (*geck huay yen*), 15 baht

RESTROOM

Squat toilet, bowl of water to flush, no paper

Best for NOODLE SOUP

Guaythiew Ta Phut

ก๋วยเตี๋ยวตาพุด, 27 หมู่ 1 (ข้ามสะพานแม่น้ำยม เลี้ยวขวาตรงไป 1.5 กม.)

27 MOO 1

This noodle stall, adjacent to the owners' house, is charming, with landscaping as pretty as any we've seen around a noodle stand. The egg noodles are still handmade each morning by the stall's original vendor, Grandpa Put, and prices remain reasonable despite the high quality of the stall's offerings.

GETTING THERE

To reach 27 Moo 1, go across the Yom River Bridge, turn right and go straight on for 1.5 km
Tel 055-682-068
Open 9.00–17.00 daily

SPECIALTY

Egg noodles with dumplings (*bamee giew*), 20–25 baht (depending on portion size)
บะหมี่เกี๊ยว

OPTIONS

- Egg noodles (*bamee*), dumplings (*giew*), wide noodles (*sen yai*), thin noodles (*sen lek*), rice vermicelli (*sen mee*), glass vermicelli (*wunsen*)
- Regular (*tamada*), spicy lemongrass (*tom yum*), Sukhothai-style (*Sukhothai*), with broth (*nam*), without broth (*hang*), without noodles (*gow low*), broth separate (*nam yaek*)

NOTABLE EXTRAS

Do-it-yourself Thai dessert (*nam khaeng sai*) bar with shaved ice, 10 baht; deep-fried dumplings (*giew tod*), 20 baht

SEATING Yes

ON THE TABLE

Chopsticks and spoons, tissues, toothpicks, condiment tray, fish sauce, chili sauce

BEVERAGES

Soft drink/carbonated beverage (*nam atlom*), 12–15 baht (depending on size); fresh water (*nam plao*), 10 baht

RESTROOM

Squat toilet, bowl of water to flush, no paper

Best for
NOODLE SOUP

Isaan

Khon Kaen · Udon Thani · Ubon Ratchathani

Isaan food once got a bad rap from many urban Thais who considered the cuisine to be "downmarket" and "primitive". However, it is this very quality—its directness and simplicity—that has made Isaan dishes some of the most popular in the country. Most major street corners in the capital feature a *som tum* (grated papaya salad) and/or grilled chicken vendor, and almost every Thai enjoys an Isaan trinity (*som tum*, grilled chicken and sticky rice) at least once a month.

While Isaan food has been sweetened and prettified for the big city, its major characteristics are spice, acidity and a light hand with the sugar. Grilling and boiling are the major cooking techniques used, thus explaining the proliferation of carts equipped with little grills and a selection of earthenware pots for the various spicy soups that, despite the sweltering heat, are very popular in this region.

Grilled chicken, Ubon Ratchathani

Breakfast in northeastern Thailand

Issan-style spicy soup

Khon Kaen

Khon Kaen is one of Thailand's fastest growing cities. Long a magnet for local business investors, it is now starting to attract the interest of tourists seeking a foothold from which to explore the Isaan region, the country's most populous region and home to its most popular regional cuisine. Characterized by strong tart, salty and spicy flavors, Isaan specialties include street food standbys like grilled chicken and grated papaya salad.

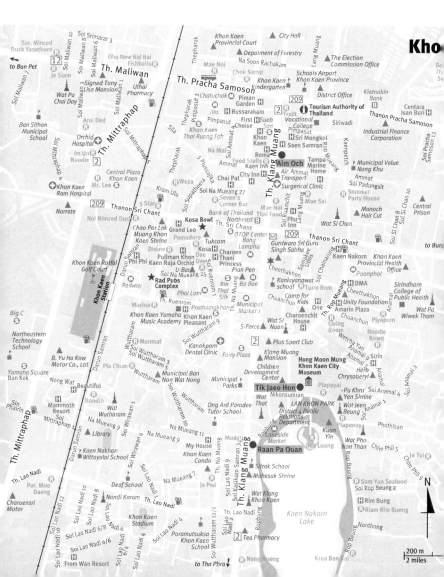

Tik Jaeo Hon

ติ๊กแจ่วฮ้อน, แยกถนนรอบบึงตัดกับนิกรสำราญ

CORNER OF ROPBUNG AND NIKONSUMRAN ROADS

Close to Kaen Nakorn Lake, this roadside joint under a tent attracts all types of patrons once the air gets cool enough to contemplate a nice hot vat of spicy-tart broth, the base for the Isaan-style sukiyaki known to locals as either *jaew hon* or *jum jim*.

GETTING THERE

Located at the corner of Ropbung and Nikonsumran Roads, close to Kaen Nakorn Lake
Tel 043-226-906
Open 17.30–23.00 daily

SPECIALTY

Sukiyaki in an Isaan-style broth with a spicy-salty dipping sauce (*jaew hon*), 29 baht (small), 100 baht (large)
อาหารแนะนำ: แจ่วฮ้อน

OPTIONS

- Pork (*moo*), beef (*nuea*), mixed (*ruam*)
- With innards (*gub krueang nai*), without innards (*mai sai krueang nai*)
- Small orders accompanied by glass vermicelli (*wunsen*), cabbage, herbs; large orders include mushrooms as well

SEATING Yes

ON THE TABLE

Burner connected to gas canister; a pot of broth is set on the burner once you are seated

BEVERAGES

Soft drink/carbonated beverage (*nam atlom*), 12–35 baht (depending on size); beer, 55–80 baht (depending on brand); fresh water (*nam plao*), 10 baht

RESTROOM No

Best for
ISAAN
DISHES

Raan Pa Ouan

ร้านป้าอ้วน, ถนนรอบบึง

ROPBUNG ROAD

This popular family-run Isaan eatery might be considered a chain, but who cares, it's that good. Aside from the usual array of grated vegetable salads (*som tum*) and grilled fish or chicken offerings, Pa Ouan also features the hard-to-find fish dish *mieng pla*.

Best for **ISAAN DISHES**

GETTING THERE

Located on Ropbung Road, facing Kaen Nakorn Lake
Tel 083-563-6763
Open 9.00–20.00 daily

SPECIALTY

Deep-fried tilapia pieces with garnishes (*mieng pla nin tod samunprai*), 200 baht
เมี่ยงปลานิลทอดสมุนไพร

NOTABLE EXTRAS

Isaan sausages (*sai grog Isaan*), 70 baht; spicy soup with pork ribs (*tom saeb gradook moo aun*), 150 baht; omelet with red ant eggs (*kai jiew kai mot dang*), available in the rainy season, 80 baht

SEATING Yes

ON THE TABLE

Tissues, toothpicks

BEVERAGES

Soft drink/carbonated beverage (*nam atlom*), 20–150 baht (depending on size); fresh water (*nam plao*), 15–25 baht (depending on size); ice, an additional 15 baht

RESTROOM Squat toilet, no paper

Kai Kratha

inspired by Aim Och

This is a great way to start the morning. We substituted ramekins for the small frying pans featured in most of the street stalls serving this dish, but if you do happen to have small pans, use them!

2 servings

You will need

2 ramekins, well-buttered
2 mini-baguettes or soft rolls (for real Thai street food flavor, they should be as sweet as possible)
butter (for toasting buns)
1 link Chinese sausage (*gunchieng*), sliced
6 slices *moo yaw* (Vietnamese steamed pork paté); baloney works with a pinch
2–4 eggs, depending on size of ramekins
salt and pepper (to taste)
fish sauce with sliced chilies, Maggi sauce or Golden Mountain sauce (to taste)
Sriracha sauce (to taste)

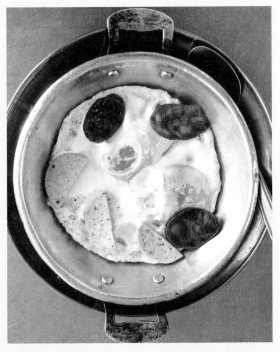

To make

1 Preheat the oven to 325 °F/180 °C.
2 Place the buns, slightly open and with their insides buttered, into a casserole and toast in the oven until warm and the edges are light brown and the butter has melted.
3 In a pan, warm slices of Chinese sausage and/or *moo yaw* until hot to the touch.
4 Crack 1–2 eggs into each buttered ramekin, depending on size. Cook in the oven for 5–10 minutes (depending on how well your oven works), until the whites are set when you jiggle them and start to pull away slightly from the sides of the ramekin. If you like your eggs to be firmer, wait at least 10 minutes.
5 Take the eggs out of the oven and garnish with the sausage and pork paté. If you have cooked minced meat and/or vegetables, scatter those on your eggs as well. Season with salt and pepper.
6 Fill the toasted buns with slices of sausage and pork paté. Serve with the eggs. Make sure to pass around the fish sauce, Maggi, sweet chili sauce and other condiments.

Aim Och

เอมโอช, ถนนกลางเมือง ตรงข้ามโรงแรมโรมา

KLANG MUANG ROAD

This place is easy to spot for its horde of customers who come for the *kai kratha*, egg in a pan garnished with Chinese sausage and Vietnamese pork paté, a mid-twentieth century invention said to have originated from Vietnam during the Vietnam War.

GETTING THERE
Located on Klang Muang Road,
across from the Roma Hotel
Tel 043-241-382, 086-630-4886
Open 4.00–13.00 daily

SPECIALTY
Egg in a pan (*kai kratha*),
20 baht; bread stuffed with
steamed pork paté and
Chinese sausage (*khanom
pang yod sai*), 15 baht a piece
ไข่กระทะ และขนมปังยัดไส้

NOTABLE EXTRAS
Pork's blood in broth (*gow
low sieng ji lued moo*), 45 baht;
rice, additional 6 baht

SEATING Yes

ON THE TABLE
Chopsticks and spoons,
tissues, bottled water,
condiment tray (pickled
pounded chilies, chili powder,
sugar, fish sauce), chili sauce,
ketchup, imitation Maggi
sauce, real Maggi sauce,
white pepper

BEVERAGES
Hot/cold coffee (*gafae ron/
yen*), hot/cold tea (*cha ron/
yen*), hot/cold Milo (*Milo
ron/yen*), hot/cold cocoa
(*coco ron/yen*), hot/cold
milk (*nom ron/yen*), 20 baht;
orange juice (*nam som*),
25 baht; fresh water (*nam
plao*), 15 baht

RESTROOM
Western toilet, no paper

Udon Thani

While Udon Thani is unlikely to be at the top of most tourists' itineraries, it does enjoy a thriving and delicious food scene. Local Isaan favorites such as grilled meats, grated salads and minced meat salads mix with Chinese-inspired street specialties like egg noodles and rice congee, as well as Thai-Vietnamese fusion dishes like *kai kratha* (egg in a pan) to create one of Thailand's most interesting showcases for street food.

Som Tum Saeb Soi Benchang

ส้มตำแซบซอยเบญจางค์, 32/15 ถนนเบญจางค์ ซอย 1 สุดถนน อยู่ฝั่งซ้าย

32/15 BENCHANG SOI 1

The pounded salads (*som tum*) here are prized by locals for their light, clear flavors, while the overall cleanliness of the eatery—a stall with a dining area—also earns high points. All is not salad-related, however; the minced pork salad also draws raves, as does the fried chicken.

GETTING THERE

Located on Benchang Soi 1, towards the end of the road on the left-hand side
Tel 081-965-1807
Open 9.00–15.00 daily

Best for
ISAAN DISHES

SPECIALTY

Grated pounded salad (*som tum*), 40 baht
ส้มตำทุกอย่าง

OPTIONS

- Spicy-tart-sweet with peanuts and dried shrimp (*Thai*)
- Pickled field crab with fermented Thai anchovies (*pu pla rah*)
- Literally "confused", a mix of whatever is on hand, such as fermented rice noodles, green papaya, fermented sour pork sausage, etc. (*mua*)
- Fermented rice noodles and green papaya (*sua*)
- Traditional central Thai-style with salted egg (*Thai kai kem*)
- "Jungle-style" with snails, bamboo shoots, fermented rice noodles, green papaya, acacia leaves, Thai eggplant (*pa*)

NOTABLE EXTRAS

Fried chicken (*gai tod*),

50 baht a piece; minced pork salad (*larb moo*), 40 baht; sticky rice (*khao niew*), 10–40 baht

SEATING Yes

ON THE TABLE

Tissues

BEVERAGES

Soft drink/carbonated beverage (*nam atlom*), 35 baht a bottle; fresh water (*nam plao*), 10 baht

RESTROOM

Squat toilet, bowl of water to flush, no paper

King Ocha
คิงส์โอชา, 22/1–2 ถนนสี่ศรัทธา

22/1–2 SI SATTHA ROAD

This packed open-air shophouse is swarming with hungry patrons
on weekends, all seeking the house specialty, *kai kratha* (egg in a pan).
The real draw here, though, is the fragrant freshly baked buns
buttered with sugar or stuffed with slivers of sausage.

GETTING THERE

Located on Si Sattha Road, near
the Haa Yaek Market. Follow the
crowds in the morning
Tel 042-343-481
Open 4.00–10.00 daily

SPECIALTY

Egg in a pan (*kai kratha*), 25
baht; buns stuffed with pork
paté and sausage (*khanom
pang yad sai*), 8 baht each
ไข่กระทะและขนมปังยัดไส้

NOTABLE EXTRAS

Rice with fried pork paté
(*khao moo yaw tod*), 35 baht

SEATING Yes

ON THE TABLE

Tissues, toothpicks, sugar

Best for **VIETNAMESE-STYLE DISHES**

cubes, salt, white pepper, ketchup, chili sauce, Maggi sauce

BEVERAGES

Hot tea water (*nam cha*), free; Chinese-style black iced coffee (*olieng*), hot/cold Thai-style tea with milk (*cha nom ron/yen*), black iced tea (*cha dum yen*), hot/cold milk (*nom ron/yen*), hot/cold Nescafe (*Nescafe ron/yen*), hot/cold Moccona (*Moccona ron/yen*), hot/cold Ovaltine (*Ovaltine ron/yen*), 15 baht; orange juice (*nam som*), 20 baht/glass, 40 baht/bottle

RESTROOM

Western toilet, bowl of water to flush, no paper

Som Tum Jae Gai
ส้มตำเจ๊ไก่, 167/15 ถนนนเรศวร
167/15 NARESUAN ROAD

For a real hit of Isaan flavor, look no further than this sprawling roadside stall, where the julienned and pounded salads are so popular that customers must take a number, deli counter-style, to place an order. A huge range of *som tum* is available.

GETTING THERE
On the left-hand side of Naresuan Road as you are come from the town center
Tel 087-373-2128, 080-762-0350
Open 8.00–15.30 daily

SPECIALTY
Lao-style grated green papaya salad with fermented anchovies (*som tum lao*), 30 baht; "jungle-style" grated salad with snails, bamboo shoots, fermented rice noodles, green papaya, acacia leaves, Thai eggplant (*som tum pa*), 35 baht.
ส้มตำลาวและส้มตำป่า

NOTABLE EXTRAS
Grilled chicken (*gai yang*), 30–120 baht (depending on size); grilled fish (*pla pow*), 120–160 baht; boiled snails (*hoy thom*), 10 baht; sticky rice (*khao niew*), 10 baht

SEATING Yes

ON THE TABLE
Tissues, toothpicks, jug of fresh water, fish sauce

BEVERAGES
Chrysanthemum tea (*geck huay*), red lotus tea (*cha bua dang*), roselle juice (*nam krajiep*), red lotus juice (*nam bua dang*), bael fruit juice (*nam matum*), punch, 25 baht; soft drink/carbonated beverage (*nam atlom*), 30 baht; fresh water (*nam plao*), 20 baht

RESTROOM
Western toilet, no paper

Best for
ISAAN
DISHES

Som Tum

inspired by Som Tum Jae Gai

Dried shrimp isn't essential to this dish, but to make a standard "Thai-style" grated salad it is important to include the peanuts.

4 servings

You will need

3 cloves garlic
1–3 bird's eye chilies
3 tbs fish sauce
juice of 2–3 limes
1 tbs palm sugar or
    granulated sugar
1 cup grated carrot
1 cup grated daikon
    radish
3 inches long beans cut
    into 5 cm pieces
3–5 cherry tomatoes
Ajinomoto (to taste,
    optional)
crushed roasted peanuts
    (for garnish)
dried small shrimp (for
    garnish)

To make

1 Using a mortar and pestle, pound the garlic with the chilies to form a paste. (Vendors call each chili a *met* and ask customers how many *met* they want in their *som tum*. Answers usually range from none (*mai sai prik*) to five (*ha*).

2 Add the fish sauce, lime juice and sugar. Taste to correct the seasoning. (This is your last chance to fix the dressing before all the other ingredients are added to the mortar.)

3 Add the carrot, daikon radish, long beans and cherry tomatoes to the mortar. Mash gently with the pestle to ensure the strands get bruised (nothing is worse than pieces that are too crunchy) while scraping the bowl with a large spoon with your other hand.

4 It's your decision to add Ajinomoto or not, but every Thai I have spoken to insists that it is an essential ingredient. We used a light sprinkling on our finished salad before garnishing with crushed roasted peanuts and dried shrimp (both to taste). A platter of fresh vegetables—sliced green beans, a wedge of cabbage and some cucumber spears—accompanies the salad. If you want to be really traditional, serve alongside sticky rice and grilled chicken or pork shoulder or, if you want to be like Jae Gai, a bowl of boiled snails.

Ubon Ratchathani

Ubon Ratchathani is blessed with a bounty of street food vendors selling perennial crowd pleasers, ranging from egg in a pan (*kai kratha*) to Thai-Vietnamese specialties, and from straight-up Isaan fare to vegetarian rice curry (*khao gub gaeng*). If you have limited time to spend in the Isaan region, you may do well to stop here since Ubon Ratchathani offers a chance to sample all of the region's street food favorites.

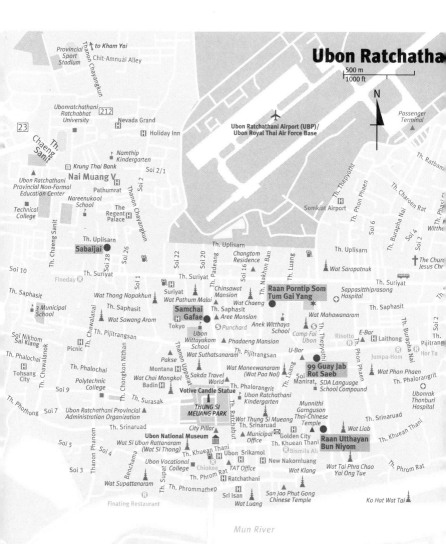

Samchai Gafae

(or Samchai Coffee) สามชัยกาแฟ, 56/58 ถนนผาแดง

56/58 PADAENG ROAD

For a taste of egg in a pan (*kai kratha*), a dish said to have originated in Vietnam where it was modeled on the American breakfast, look no further than this bustling coffee shop. Besides *kai kratha*, you can also get old-fashioned Thai-style coffee sweetened with condensed milk.

GETTING THERE

Look for the bustling spot on Padaeng Road, south of the airport, in the morning
Tel 045-209-118, 045-240-241
Open 5.30–13.30 daily

SPECIALTY
Egg in a pan (*kai kratha*), 30 baht
ไข่กระทะ

NOTABLE EXTRAS
Chinese rice porridge (*jok*), 25 baht or 30 baht with egg; pork's blood in broth (*thom lued moo*), 35 baht; buns stuffed with pork paté and sausage (*khanom pang yad sai*), 10 baht

SEATING Yes

ON THE TABLE
Tisues, toothpicks, bottled water, condiment tray, fish sauce, chili sauce, ketchup, Maggi sauce, white pepper, salt

BEVERAGES
Old-fashioned coffee (*gafae boran*), old-fashioned tea (*cha boran*), hot milk (*nom ron*), orange juice (*nam som*), 20 baht; Chinese-style black iced coffee (*olieng*), Nescafe, Milo, black iced tea (*cha dum yen*), cold milk (*nom yen*), soft drink/carbonated beverage (*nam atlom*), 15 baht

RESTROOM
Squat toilet, no paper

Order a side of Chinese sausage to go with the jok.

Best for VIETNAMESE-STYLE DISHES

99 Guay Jab Rot Saeb

99 ก๋วยจั๊บรสแซบ, หัวมุมสี่แยกไฟแดงถนนพิชิตรังสรรค์ ตัดกับถนนเทพโยธี

CORNER OF TEPYOTHI AND PIJITRANGSAN ROADS

An unassuming shophouse that turns out a suspiciously delicious-smelling
broth hiding thick rice noodles known in Thailand as *guay jab Yuan*—
a Vietnamese-inspired version of Chinese hand-rolled rice noodles.

GETTING THERE

Located on the corner of Tepyothi
and Pijitrangsan Roads
Tel 045-260-424
Open 13.00–22.00 daily

SPECIALTY
Vietnamese-style Chinese
noodles in pork broth
(*guay jab Yuan*), 35–60 baht
(depending on options)
ก๋วยจั๊บญวน

OPTIONS
- Minced pork (*moo deng*)
- Chicken wings (*pik gai*)
- Chicken feet (*theen gai*)
- Pig's blood (*lued moo*)
- Pig's bones (*gradook moo*)
- Mixed (*ruam*)

SEATING Yes

ON THE TABLE
Tissues, bottled water, jug
of fresh water, fish sauce,
roasted chili paste, pickled
chilies in vinegar

BEVERAGES
Carrot juice (*nam* carrot),
orange juice (*nam som*),
punch, 15 baht; soft drink/
carbonated beverage (*nam
atlom*), coconut juice (*nam
maphrao*), pineapple juice
(*nam saparot*), 12 baht;
chrysanthemum tea (*geck
huay*), pennywort juice (*nam

bai bua bok), roselle juice
(*nam krajiep*), black herbal
jelly juice (*chow guay*), longan
juice (*nam lamyai*), tamarind
juice (*nam makham*), 10 baht

RESTROOM
Squat toilet, bowl of water
to flush, no paper

Best for NOODLE SOUP

Sabaijai

สบายใจ, 413/3 ถนนอุปลีสาน

413/3 UPLISARN ROAD

Sabaijai bears testament to the sizable community of Thai-Vietnamese in the area, descended from people who fled from neighboring Vietnam during the war. Its menu is long and chock-full of little-seen dishes, but the stand-outs are the spring rolls and Vietnamese dumplings (*naem nueng*).

GETTING THERE

On a major road bordering the southern end of the airport
Tel 045-242-581, 087-650-9167, 083-598-3246
Open 8.00–18.00 daily

Best for VIETNAMESE-STYLE DISHES

SPECIALTY

Vietnamese dumplings (*naem nueng*), 70–100 baht (depending on size)
แหนมเนือง

NOTABLE EXTRAS

Fried spring rolls (*mieng tod*), Fresh spring rolls (*mieng sod*), 30 baht each

SEATING Yes

ON THE TABLE

Tissues, bottled water, condiment tray

BEVERAGES

Chrysanthemum tea (*geck huay*), black herbal juice (*chow guay*), roselle juice (*nam krajiep*), carrot juice (*nam* carrot), soft drink/carbonated beverage (*nam atlom*), fresh water (*nam plao*), 10 baht; Leo beer, 55 baht

RESTROOM

Squat toilet, bowl of water to flush, no paper

141

Raan Porntip Som Tum Gai Yang
ร้านพรทิพย์ส้มตำไก่ย่าง, ถนนสรรพสิทธิ์

SAPHASIT ROAD

No visit to Ubon is complete without a meal at this basic stall next to the road, now much more like a restaurant than a stall, complete with a *guay jab* stall 16.00–20.00 daily. The specialty, of course, is Isaan food: grated salads (*som tum*), grilled chicken (*gai yang*) and sticky rice (*khao niew*).

GETTING THERE
Halfway along Saphasit Road, one of Ubon's busier roads
Tel 089-720-8101
Open 6.00–20.00 daily

SPECIALTY
Grated green papaya salad (*som tum Thai*), 40 baht; grilled chicken (*gai yang*), 90–100 baht/half, 180 baht/whole; sticky rice (*khao niew*), 10 baht
ส้มตำไทย ไก่ย่าง ข้าวเหนียว

NOTABLE EXTRAS
Fried chicken (*gai tod*), 90–180 baht; Isaan-style minced pork salad (*larb moo*), 60 baht; grated papaya salad with fermented Thai anchovy (*som tum pla rah*), 30 baht

SEATING Yes

ON THE TABLE
Tissues, straws, bottled water

BEVERAGES
Soft drink/carbonated beverage (*nam atlom*), 15–20 baht; Chang beer, 50 baht; Leo beer, 60 baht; Singha beer, 70 baht; Heineken beer, 80 baht ; fresh water (*nam plao*), 10 baht;

RESTROOM
Squat toilet, bowl of water to flush, no paper

Best for ISAAN DISHES

Raan Utthayan Bun Niyom

ร้านอุทยานบุญนิยม, สี่แยกถนนเทพโยธีตัดกับถนนศรีณรงค์

CORNER OF THEPYOTHI AND SRINARUAD ROADS

Vegetarian heaven is here, thanks to a group of volunteers who make daily treks to this roadside canteen to cook up a panoply of curries, salads and desserts for a dedicated group of customers. A general store selling a selection of eco-friendly items is also on the restaurant grounds.

GETTING THERE

Located at the corner of Thepyothi
and Srinaruad Roads near a temple
Tel 086-871-1580
Open 6.00–14.00 daily except
Monday

SPECIALTY

Vegetarian curries with rice
10 baht (one curry),15 baht
(two curries), 20 baht (three
curries)
ข้าวราดแกงเจ

NOTABLE EXTRAS

Vegetarian noodles, 15–20
baht (depending on size);
vegetarian grated papaya
salad, 15 baht

SEATING Yes

ON THE TABLE

Nothing

BEVERAGES

Soy coffee, chrysanthemum
tea (*geck huay*), iced milk tea
(*cha yen*), taro milk, tamarind
juice (*nam makham*),
passionfruit juice (*nam
saowarot*), roselle juice (*nam*

krajiep), bael fruit juice (*nam
matum*), mushroom juice,
pandanus juice (*nam bait*oey),
sweet grass juice, butterfly
pea juice (*nam dok anchan*),
all 10 baht

TOILET

Squat toilet, bowl of water
to flush, no paper

The South

Phuket · Cha-Am · Hua Hin

Sand and sun: these are the two words most commonly associated with the south of Thailand. Indeed, much of southern Thai food reflects the abundance of its sea life: a variety of freshly grilled or deep-fried seafood, spicy clear soups featuring fresh fish and prawns and coconut milk-based curries rich in crab, fish and wild ginger.

Southern Thailand is also home to large Thai-Chinese and Thai-Muslim communities, as evidenced by the street food. Steamed dumplings, biryanis and soup noodles are commonly available at roadside vendors. Phuket also boasts a unique range of street food dishes inspired by the Hokkien Chinese who settled there.

Fried chicken wings

Khanom jeen with curry

Khanom jeen relishes

Pork noodles

Phuket

Phuket is an interesting case study in street food. Although a part of Thailand, the island paradise can perhaps claim more culinary ties with neighboring Malaysia. Featuring a mélange of Malay-influenced Thai-Muslim and Hokkien Chinese cuisines with a hearty dose of fiery Thai-style chili dishes, Phuket's street food offers visitors a chance to savor dishes unavailable elsewhere in the country. Start with stir-fried Hokkien-style noodles topped with fried egg, or Hokkien-style oyster omelets sprinkled with deep-fried pork rinds. The brave at heart may also want to try *lo-ba*, or deep-fried pork intestines.

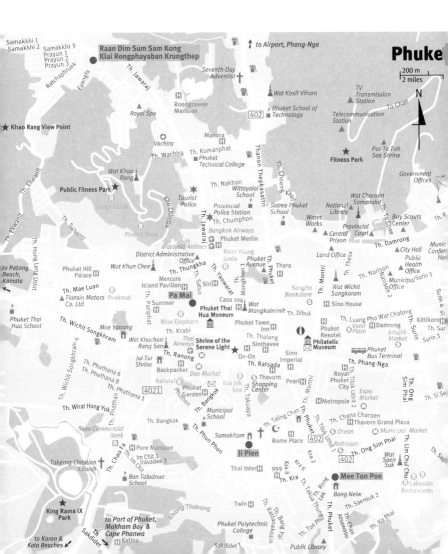

Raan Dim Sum Sam Kong Klai Rongphayaban Krungthep

ร้านติ่มซำสามกอง ใกล้โรงพยาบาลกรุงเทพ, ถนนสามกอง

SAM GONG ROAD

It's hard to believe that this place doesn't have a name. Instead, it is referred to by the frustratingly vague moniker *raan khanom jeeb glai rong ban* or "the dim sum place near the hospital". Luckily, the specialty here isn't so vague—delicious (and cheap) dim sum.

GETTING THERE
Located on Sam Gong Road, down the street from the Bangkok Hospital Phuket
Tel 076-210-977
Open 6.00–11.30 daily

Best for SNACKS

SPECIALTY
Dim sum, 10 baht (small plates); 15 baht (big plates)
ติ่มซำ

OPTIONS
A tray of dim sum (steamed dumplings, chicken wings, steamed buns, etc.) is deposited on the table. Empty plates are counted, those left untouched are not

SEATING Yes

ON THE TABLE
Forks, dipping bowls, tissues, toothpicks, bottled water, tea water, chili dipping sauce, Sriracha sauce

BEVERAGES
Fresh water (*nam plao*), 10 baht

RESTROOM
Squat toilet, no paper

Mee Ton Poe

หมี่ต้นโพธ, 214/7–8 ถนนภูเก็ต ตลาดใหญ่

214/7–89 PHUKET ROAD, TALADYAI

This noodle shop is famous throughout the island for its Hokkien-style fried noodles (*mee pad Hokkien*) topped with shallots and pork cracklings. A less famous but no less delicious dish is the staff meal served just before noon. Call ahead of time and they will save you some.

GETTING THERE

Located on 214/7–89 Phuket Road, Taladyai, near a gas station
Tel 076-216-293
Open 10.30–18.00 daily except the 29th of every month

Best for **FRIED NOODLES**

SPECIALTY

Hokkien-style fried noodles (*mee pad Hokkien*) 40–70 baht (depending on portion size and options)
หมี่ผัดฮกเกี้ยน

OPTIONS

- With pork (*moo*), chicken (*gai*), fish (*pla*), mix of all three (*ruam*)
- With or without egg (*kai/ mai kai*)

SEATING Yes

ON THE TABLE

Chopsticks, tissues, tooth-picks, bottled water, vinegar, white pepper, chili powder, sugar

BEVERAGES

Iced coffee (*gafae yen*), iced Chinese-style black tea (*olieng*), iced tea (*cha yen*), iced black tea (*cha dum yen*), chrysanthemum tea (*geck huay*), roselle juice (*nam grajieb*), 15 baht; guava juice (*nam farang*), iced Nescafe (*Nescafe yen*), 20 baht; iced fresh coffee (*kafae sod yen*), iced chocolate (*chocolate yen*), 25 baht

RESTROOM

Squat toilet, bowl of water to flush, paper outside

Ji Pien

ร้านอาหาร โอวต้าวจี้เปี่ยน้, ซอยพูนผล 7 ถนนตะกั่วป่า

SOI PHOOPHOL 7, TAKUAPA ROAD

This 80-year-old roadside stall is among one of the oldest on the island. It has moved location over the years but there's one constant: its specialty, a Hokkien dish known as *o-tao*, an oyster omelet topped with cubed taro and pork cracklings.

GETTING THERE

Located off Takuapa Road, on Soi Phoonphol 7
Tel 084-062-1232
Open 17.00–23.00 daily

SPECIALTY

Hokkien-style oyster omelet (*o-tao*), 35–70 baht (depending on toppings)
โอต้าว (หอยนางรมทอดแบบ
ฮกเกี้ยน)

OPTIONS

- Regular (*tamada*) with one egg
- Special (*piset*) with two eggs
- Extra oysters (*piset hoy*) with shrimp and squid (*piset perm goong gub pla muk*)
- Vegetarian (*jay*)

SEATING Yes

ON THE TABLE

Chopsticks, forks and spoons, tissues, tea water, pickled garnishes for *khanom jeen*, eggs, vinegar, fish sauce, chili powder, sugar

BEVERAGES

Black iced tea (*cha dum yen*), bottled water, 10 baht; soft drink/carbonated beverage (*nam atlom*), 12 baht

RESTROOM No

Best for
SNACKS

Pa Mai

ป้ามัย, แยกหัวมุมถนนสตูลตัดกับดีบุก ใกล้โรงเรียนปลูกปัญญา

INTERSECTION OF SAGUL AND DIBUK ROADS

If you have time to go to only one place while in Phuket, make sure it's this one. While some gourmets will claim fish meatballs are Phuket's main specialty, the most sought-after dish here actually is fermented rice noodles in a coconut milk-based seafood sauce (*khanom jeen nam ya*).

GETTING THERE

Located at the intersection of Sagul and Dibuk Roads, near Wittaya School
Tel 076-258-037
Open 7.00–12.00 daily

Best for FERMENTED RICE NOODLES

SPECIALTY

Fermented rice noodles with crab/fish curry (*khanom jeen nam ya pu/pla*), 30 baht
ขนมจีนน้ำยาปู/ปลา

OPTIONS

The selection of curries at the front, ladled out by the server, usually includes:

- Crab and fish curries (*nam ya pu and pla*)
- Green chicken curry (*kiew waan gai*)
- Beef curry (*nua*)
- Sweet curry (*nam prik*)
- Southern Thai fish entrails curry (*trai pla*)
- Shrimp paste dip (*nam prik kapi*)

NOTABLE EXTRAS

Steamed fish curry (*hor mok*), 15 baht

SEATING Yes

ON THE TABLE

Tissues, toothpicks, tea water, pickled greens, bean sprouts, lotus stems, cabbage, baby garlic, dried fish, soft- boiled eggs 7 baht each; cucumber salad (*ajad*), fresh and boiled vegetables, fish sauce, dried chilies, chili powder, sugar

BEVERAGES

Chinese-style black iced coffee (*olieng*), hot/cold coffee (*gafae ron/yen*), hot/cold tea (*cha ron/yen*), Ovaltine, hot/cold milk (*nom ron/yen*), hot/cold soy milk (*nom tua lueang*), 18 baht; hot black coffee (*gafae dum ron*), black iced tea (*cha dum yen*), 7 baht

RESTROOM

Western toilet, no paper

Yong's Green Beef Curry

inspired by Pa Mai

While there is no chance of obtaining Pa Mai's green curry recipe, I do have my aunt's recipe and it's made from scratch! The recipe assumes that the coconut milk used is the canned variety, which is topped by coconut cream covering the thinner, lighter milk. If your milk is not separated into cream and juice, simply thin the milk designated as "tail" milk with water (half-milk, half-water is a good rule of thumb).

4 servings

You will need

- 1 kg stewing beef with the fat kept on, cut to desired sized pieces
- 1 kg coconut milk, separated into "head" (thick creamy top) and "tail" (watery juice)
- 2 tbs galangal, chopped
- 1 tbs kaffir lime rind, chopped
- 1 tbs salt
- 3 tbs lemongrass, sliced
- ¼ cup *prik chee fah*, or green Thai chilies
- 1 tbs bird's eye chilies (leave some for garnish)
- 1½ cups shallots, sliced
- ½ cup garlic, chopped
- 2 tbs wild ginger (*grachai*)
- 1 tbs shrimp paste
- spice mix (3 tbs nutmeg, 3 tbs mace, 1 tbs coriander seeds, ½ tbs cumin)
- 2–3 tbs palm sugar
- 1 cup holy basil
- ½ cup baby eggplant (optional, as it tends to water down the curry)
- 4–5 kaffir lime leaves, torn (for garnish, optional)

To make

1. Stew the beef in coconut milk "tail" for one hour.
2. To make the paste, pound the galangal, kaffir lime rind and salt in a mortar and pestle.
3. Add the lemongrass to the mortar.
4. Add the chilies, omitting the bird's eye chilies if you don't want it too hot.
5. Add the shallots, garlic and wild ginger.
6. Add the shrimp paste.
7. Heat the finished paste in a pan with a couple of ladles of coconut milk used to stew the beef.
8. Add the spice mix (nutmeg, mace, coriander seeds and cumin).
9. Wait for the coconut milk to break and the oil to reach the surface.
10. Add a few more ladles of coconut milk until you get the desired consistency.
11. Then add the meat and coconut milk "head".
12. Add the palm sugar.
13. Add the basil and baby eggplants, if using.
14. Garnish with chilies and kaffir lime leaves.
15. Eat with roti (like its Indian namesake, but flakier), *khanom jeen* (fermented rice noodles) or, if you prefer, pickled ginger.

Cha-Am and Hua Hin

A popular weekend destination for Thais, Cha-Am and Hua Hin are a mere two and a half hours' drive south of Bangkok, making these towns two of the most accessible destinations for a Bangkok-based traveler desperate to reach the beach. Besides the obvious attractions of sun, sand and fresh seafood, Cha-am and Hua Hin also boast popular Chinese-style noodle shops, traditional Thai dessert vendors and delicious deep-fried snacks, not to mention a burgeoning night market scene.

Cha-Am

200 m

Comfort Hotel Buri

Cha-am Khun Ying Nueang Buri School

Springfield Beach Resort

District Office

Municipal Administration

Thanon Narathip

Public Library

Je Dang

Wutthisan Suksa School

Kwan Had

Top Charoen

The Regent

Municipal 1 School

Dr. Samran Clinic

Cha-am Market

Namjitr

Holiday Inn

Kluay Tod Jae Muay

Lao-Ti Yaowarat Noodle

First and Few

Ban Cha-am Station

Th. Phetkasem

to Bangkok

4

Cha Am

Wat Neren Chararam

Khao Yai

Wat Nong Chaeng

3203

Wat Rat Charoen Tham

Sondet Phra Sangharinatniont Sak Phra

1001

1001

The Imperial Lake View Resort

4

Phraratchaniwet Camp

Huai Sai Nuea

1001

Springfield Village

1010

Hua Hin

200 m

Lertros Patchana

Bank of Ayudhya

Chiang Fishball

Dune

Nai Pew Duck Noodle

Leelawadee Thai Massage & Spa

Cafe Amazon

Ban Itsara

Baan Khrai Wang

Park Saeng Thai House Seafood

You Yen

Rung Pai

Baan Suksiri

Jai Samarn Hua Hin Church

Baan Iammueang

Hai Piang

Tananchai

The Hen

Green Gallery Bed & Breakfast

Amarcord

Krua Tong Mamuang

Baan Suriya

Guaythiew Pla Nai Hoi

Semthawin School

Je Yin Somtam

Hua Hin Place

Putahracsa

Rung Napa Seafood

Nong May

Pueak

Lok

Darun Suksa School

Rajabhat Phetchaburi University

Sofitel Centara

Cups & Comp

Chomsin

1010

Gulf of Thailan

Th. Khlong Cholaprathan

Th. Phetkasem

Hai Kahardi

Palm Hill Golf

Hua Hin Airport

PHETCHABURI

PRACHUAP KIRI KHAN

Hua Hin School

Minivans to Bangkok

Lotchong Singapore Nai Dam

Khanom Wan Ban Pa Prang

Th. Chom Sin

Araya Chalelarn

Chaloem Phrakiat Park

Niranrat Tailor-Beauty Salon Training

Buchabun Art & Crafts Collection

King's Home

Black Mountain Golf Club

Klai Kangwon Palace

Hua Hin Driving

Chatchai Market

Hua Hin Adventure Tour

Sand Inn

Thai Boxing Garden

Wat Khao Noi

Le Bayburi De Pran

Night Market

Baan Manthana

Subhamitra

Hua Hin

Nicha Suite

Rajana

3218

3218

Wat Hua Hin

Gems Cha-am

Cha-ba Chalet

Euro City

Tanawit

City Beach

N

Banyan Resort

Th. Damnoen Kasem

Golf Inn

Jed Pee

San Nong

Paolo

Royal Hua Hin Golf Course

Hua Hin Station

Statue of Pone Kingpetch

1004

1043

2km

2miles

Cha-Am & Hua Hi

Namjitr

นำจิตต์ ก๋วยเตี๋ยวหมู, สามแยกไฟฟ้าชะอำ (หลังร้านเจ๊ม่วย)

AT THE THREE-WAY INTERSECTION TRAFFIC LIGHTS, CHA-AM,
BEHIND KLUAY TOD JAE MUAY

A favorite stop for Cha-am and Hua Hin-bound travelers, the 30-year-old Namjitr stall serves delicious pork noodles in a surprisingly mild spicy lemongrass (*tom yum*) broth that comes garnished with a signature ingredient: delicately blanched baby asparagus.

GETTING THERE

Located at the three-way intersection traffic lights in Cha-am, behind Kluay Tod Jae Muay
Tel 032-471-104
Open 7.30–15.30 daily

Best for **PORK NOODLE SOUP**

SPECIALTY
Noodles with pork in a spicy lemongrass (*tom yum*) broth with baby asparagus, 30–50 baht (depending on options)
ก๋วยเตี๋ยวหมูต้มยำใส่หน่อไม้ฝรั่ง

OPTIONS
- Wide noodles (*sen yai*), thin noodles (*sen lek*), rice vermicelli (*sen mee*), egg noodles (*bamee*), dumplings (*giew*)
- Pork (*moo*) or tofu (*taohu*)
- Regular pork bone broth (*nam*), spicy lemongrass broth (*tom yum*), red fermented tofu noodles (*yen ta fo*), without broth (*hang*), without noodles (*gow low*)
- Baby asparagus (*naw mai farang*) or bean sprouts (*tua ngok*), 5 baht

SEATING Yes

ON THE TABLE
Tissues, toothpicks, bottled water, chilies, fish sauce, vinegar, chili powder, pounded chilies in vinegar, sugar

BEVERAGES
Chinese-style black iced coffee (*olieng*), iced milk tea (*cha yen*), iced lemon tea (*cha manao*), chrysanthemum tea (*geck huay*), bael fruit juice (*nam matum*), soft drink/carbonated beverage (*nam atlom*), 10 baht; Splash, 12 baht; big bottle of soft drink, 35 baht; fresh water (*nam plao*), 7–15 baht

RESTROOM
Two urinals, squat toilet, bowl of water to flush, no paper

155

Kluay Tod Jae Muay

กล้วยทอดเจ๊ม่วย, สามแยกไฟฟ้าชะอำ (หน้าร้านนำจิตต์)

AT THE THREE-WAY INTERSECTION TRAFFIC LIGHTS, CHA-AM,
IN FRONT OF NAMJITR

Blink and you'll miss this deep-fried banana vendor, who plies her
trade on a streetside corner with a single large wok and bag of
bananas behind her. The ingredients of her batter are a secret
but the deliciousness of her crispy fried treats are not.

GETTING THERE

Located at the three-way
intersection traffic lights in Cha-am,
in front of Namjitr
Tel 032-471-104
Open 12.00–15.00 daily

SPECIALTY
Deep-fried bananas
(*gluay tod*), 20 baht a bag
กล้วยทอด

SEATING No

BEVERAGES No

RESTROOM No

Best for
SNACKS

Guaythiew Pla Nai Hoi

ก๋วยเตี๋ยวปลานายหอย, ถนนเลียบคลองชลประทาน ในบริเวณหมู่บ้านเขาน้อย

ALONGSIDE LIEB KHLONG CHON PRATAN, KHAO NOI, HUA HIN

This fish noodle specialty attracts locals and tourists alike at lunchtime, making it a sure bet for some ultra-hot and sweaty noshing. Luckily, the staff are efficient and experienced and drinks are plentiful.

Best for **FISH NOODLE SOUP**

Try the deep-fried fish skin!

GETTING THERE

Located alonside Lieb Khlong Chon Pratan in Khao Noi neighborhood
Tel 032-513-185
Open 10.00–15.00 daily

SPECIALTY

Fish noodles (*guaythiew pla*), 35–40 baht (depending on portion size)
ก๋วยเตี๋ยวปลา

OPTIONS

- Wide noodles (*sen yai*), thin noodles (*sen lek*), rice vermicelli (*sen mee*)
- With broth (*nam*), without broth (*hang*)

NOTABLE EXTRAS

Dumplings with fish noodles (*giew sen pla*), 35–40 baht (depending on size); deep-fried fish skin (*nung pla*), 30–50 baht (depending on size)

SEATING   Yes

ON THE TABLE

Chopsticks and spoons, tissues, toothpicks, bottled water, tea water, condiment tray, fish sauce

BEVERAGES

Old-fashioned coffee (*gafae boran*), 15 baht; orange juice

(*nam som*), 10 baht; soft drink/carbonated beverage (*nam atlom*), fresh water (*nam plao*), 9 baht;

RESTROOM

Two Western toilets, no paper

Nai Pew Duck Noodle

(Guaythiew) นายปิวก๋วยเตี๋ยวเป็ด, บนถนนเพชรเกษม ตรงข้ามปากซอยหัวหินซอย 45

PETCHKASEM ROAD

Go early if you want to snag your own table at this very popular
duck noodle stall, considered the best in a town brimming with
duck noodle vendors. Here, the duck is juicy, the noodles are
properly al dente and the broth is flavorsome.

GETTING THERE

Located on Petchkasem Road,
across the street from the entrance
to Hua Hin Soi 45
Tel 032-511-377
Open 8.00—until sold out, daily
except public holidays

Best for
DUCK NOODLE SOUP

SPECIALTY
Duck noodles (*guaythiew ped*)
40–70 baht (depending on
options)
ก๋วยเตี๋ยวเป็ด

OPTIONS
- Wide noodles (*sen yai*),
  thin noodles (*sen lek*),
  rice vermicelli (*sen mee*),
  egg noodles (*bamee*),

  dumplings (*giew*),
  bamee and *giew*, more
  noodles (*sen pum*), more
  congealed duck blood
  (*lued pum*)
- Duck leg (*ka ped*), congealed duck blood (*lued*),
  extra duck meat (*ped pum*)
- With broth (*nam*), without
  broth (*hang*), without
  noodles (*gow low*)

NOTABLE EXTRAS
Deep-fried pork mousse
(*tod mun moo*), 30 baht

SEATING Yes

ON THE TABLE
Chopsticks, spoons, toothpicks,
bottled water, fish sauce,
chilies, chilies in vinegar, chili

powder, garlic cloves, sugar,
Golden Mountain sauce

BEVERAGES
Sugarcane juice (*nam tansot*),
roselle juice (*nam krajiep*),
tamarind juice (*nam
makham*), bael fruit juice
(*nam matum*), soft drink/
carbonated beverage (*nam
atlom*), 10–15 baht; fresh
water (*nam plao*), 10 baht;
Splash, 12 baht

RESTROOM
Squat toilet, bowl of water
to flush, no paper

Khanom Wan Ban Pa Prang

ขนมหวานบ้านป้าปรางค์, 25 หัวหินซอย 55

25 HUA HIN SOI 55

The wide range of traditional Thai sweets—an assortment of dumplings, usually sticky rice flour-based, floating in savory coconut milk—is what draws dozens of customers to this unassuming spot in the middle of Hua Hin town. Once strictly takeout, it has since added three tables.

GETTING THERE

Close to the morning market in Hua Hin Soi 55, on the right-hand side from the main road
Tel 032-512-611
Open 11.00—until sold out, daily

SPECIALTY

Traditional Thai sweets in coconut milk, 15 baht a bowl
ขนมหวานแบบไทยๆ ใส่กะทิ
เช่น ข้าวฟ่าง ขนมโค และสาคู

OPTIONS

- Young sticky rice mash in coconut milk (*khao fang*)
- Black beans in coconut milk (*tua dum*)
- Black sticky rice drizzled in coconut milk (*khao niew dum*)
- Yellow beans in coconut milk (*thao suan*)
- Tapioca pearls with coconut and jackfruit in coconut milk (*sakult*)
- Pumpkin in coconut milk (*fuk tong gaeng buat*)
- Rice flour "noodles" in sweet and savory coconut milk (*kai thao*)
- Boiled bananas in coconut milk (*gluay buat chee*)
- Bananas in syrup (*gluay chuem*)
- Rice flour dumplings stuffed with coconut in coconut milk (*khanom ko*)

Best for **DESSERTS**

SEATING Yes

ON THE TABLE
Nothing

BEVERAGES
Free fresh water in the back

RESTROOM No

Lotchong Singapore Nai Dam

ลอดช่องสิงคโปร์นายดำ, หัวหินซอย 55 ใกล้สี่แยก

HUA HIN SOI 55, AT THE FOUR-WAY INTERSECTON

There are few surprises at this vendor on the edge of a food court, except for the excellent version of *lotchong Singapore* (sticky rice flour-based green noodles with jackfruit with shaved ice and coconut milk). It is served to go in a handy plastic cup with an extra-wide straw.

GETTING THERE

On Hua Hin Soi 55, a few feet from Khanom Wan Ban Pa Prang
Tel 081-922-7120
Open 10.00–17.00 daily

SPECIALTY
Singapore-style sticky rice flour-based "noodles" (*lotchong Singapore*), 15–20 baht (depending on container, size or seating)
ลอดช่องสิงคโปร์

SEATING Yes (in food court)

ON THE TABLE
Nothing

BEVERAGES No

RESTROOM No

Best for
DESSERTS

List of Stalls by Food Type

DESSERTS
Bua Loy Som Wang Song Khreuang
  ___ngkok) *44*
  jit (Bangkok) *33*
  nom Wan Ban Pa Prang (Hua
  ꞏ-Iin) *159*
Lotchong Singapore (Bangkok) *36*
Lotchong Singapore Nai Dam
  (Cha-Am) *160*
Nam Kaeng Sai Khun Muk
  (Bangkok) *78*
Raan Khao Niew Mamuang
  (Bangkok) *79*
Seng Sim Ee (Bangkok) *63*

EGG IN A PAN (KAI KRATHA)
Aim Och (Khon Kaen) *130*
King Ocha (Udon Thani) *134*
Sabaijai (Ubon Ratchathani)*141*

EGG NOODLES
Bamee Gua (Bangkok) *84*
Bamee Sawang (Bangkok) *57*
Bamee Slow (Bangkok) *74*
Bamee Soi 38 (Bangkok) *83*

FERMENTED RICE NOODLES
Khanom Jeen Nam Ngeaw Pa Suk
  (Chiang Rai) *114*
Pa Mai (Phuket) *152*

FRIED NOODLES
Hoy Tod Chaolay (Bangkok) *73*
Jae Fai (Bangkok) *48*
Jae Ouan Rad Na Yod Pak
  (Bangkok) *32*
Mee Ton Poe (Phuket) *150*
Nai Peng Potchana (Bangkok) *60*
Pad Thai Fai Luk (Bangkok) *76*
Thipsamai Noodle Shop (Bangkok)
  52
Xie Shark Fin (Bangkok) *31*

ISAAN DISHES
Gai Tod Thiengkheun (Chiang Mai)
  108
Jay Ouan Moo Jum (Bangkok) *66*
Polo Fried Chicken (Bangkok) *71*

Raan Pa Ouan (Khon Kaen) *128*
Raan Porntip Som Tum Gai Yang
  (Ubon Ratchathani) *142*
Som Tum Jae Gai (Udon Thani) *136*
Som Tum Saeb Soi Benchang
  (Udon Thani) *133*
Tik Jaeo Hon (Khon Kaen) *127*

RICE
Gai Tawn Prathunam (Bangkok) *89*
Jib Gi Ped Yang (Bangkok) *54*
Khao Mok Gai Convent (Bangkok)
  65
Kiet Ocha (Chiang Mai) *102*
Ko Jua Huad (Bangkok) *55*
Nai Jui (Bangkok) *30*
Rot Thip Yod Pak (Baan Mo)
  (Bangkok) *47*
Sri Morakot (Bangkok) *59*

RICE PORRIDGE
Jok Moo on 38 (Bangkok) *77*
Jok Samyan (Bangkok) *62*
Khao Tom Bowon (Bangkok) *43*
Sieng Gi (Bangkok) *40*
Than Ngi Hwood (Bangkok) *34*

SNACKS
Chongki (Bangkok) *58*
Guaythiew Lod (Bangkok) *29*
Ji Pien (Phuket) *151*
Kangi Nam Tao Thong (Bangkok)
  38
Kluay Tod Jae Muay (Cha-Am) *156*
Nai Mong Hoy Tod (Bangkok) *37*
Patongko Sawoei (Bangkok) *45*
Raan Dim Sum Sam Kong Klai
  Rongphayaban Krungthep
  (Phuket) *149*
Samosa (Bangkok) *41*
Tur Ca Co (Chiang Mai) *107*
Yaowapa (Chiang Mai) *106*

SOUP NOODLES
99 Guay Jab Rot Saeb (Ubon
  Rathchathani) *140*
Anamai (Bangkok) *85*
Chia Duck Noodles (Bangkok) *88*

Guay Jab Nam Khon Sam Kasat
  (Chiang Mai) *98*
Guay Jab Ouan Pochana (Bangkok)
  35
Guaythiew Hear Sung (Chiang Mai)
  100
Guaythiew Pik Gai Sai Nampheung
  (Bangkok) *81*
Guaythiew Pla Nai Hoi (Hua Hin)
  157
Guaythiew Ta Phut (Sukhothai) *122*
Guaythiew Ta Pui (Sukhothai) *121*
JC Yen Ta Fo (Bangkok) *68*
Khao Soi Islam (Chiang Rai) *112*
Khao Soi Islam (Lampang) *118*
Khao Soi Lamduan Faham (Chiang
  Mai) *104*
Khao Soi Samerjai (Chiang Mai) *93*
Khrua Nai Soi (Bangkok) *46*
Lim Lao Ngo (Bangkok) *39*
Nai Pew Duck Noodle (Hua Hin) *158*
Namjitr (Cha-Am) *155*
New Chu Ros (Bangkok) *50*
Niyom Pochana (Lampang) *117*
Nuea Wua Rot Yiem (Chiang Rai)
  111
Raan Guaythiew Tamleung (Chiang
  Mai) *96*
Rungrueang (Bangkok) *80*
Sa-Ard (Chiang Mai) *103*
Saew (Bangkok) *82*
Somsong Pochana (Bangkok) *51*
Yen Ta Fo Sri Ping (Chiang Mai) *95*

SUKIYAKI
Elvis Suki (Bangkok) *86*

VEGETARIAN DISHES
Raan Jae Yai (Chiang Mai) *109*
Raan Utthayan Bun Niyom (Ubon
  Ratchathani) *144*

VIETNAMESE-STYLE DISHES
Aim Och (Khon Kaen) *130*
King Ocha (Udon Thani) *134*
Sabaijai (Ubon Ratchathani) *141*
Samchai Gafae (Ubon Ratchathani)
  139

About the Author

Chawadee Nualkhair has lived in Thailand on and off since 1995. She presently lives in Bangkok with her husband and two children. Formerly a financial journalist at Reuters, she now writes freelance, mainly about food. She enjoys all types of fried noodles but admits she is not a big fan of *jok* (rice porridge).

Acknowledgments

Many people helped in the making of this book. First and foremost, my family and husband Win, who were unfailingly patient and always willing to risk stomach and limb while accompanying me on my many "research" trips around the country; Karen Blumberg, whose support and photos were invaluable; Fah Sakharet and Jason Michael Lang, whose beautiful work made this book possible; Jennifer Chen and Alan Cooper, who helped shape something coherent out of my many words; Chris Schultz, whose cooking expertise helped with every recipe; Janet Brown, who helped give me a reason for writing those words; Winner Dachpian, whose guidance helped fill these pages; and Noy Thrupkaew, without whose advice there would not be a book.